I dedicate this book to you.

I know you are going through so much.

God loves you.

You will make it through.

I promise.

~ Table of Contents ~

So where do I begin? I wanted to write an introduction to the book that would help set the tone for the testimony you are about to read. My testimony began twenty-seven years ago when I met my ex-husband. I have remained unspoken about the pain and hurt that I have been through. I have kept to myself regarding the immeasurable amount of destructive actions that have come against me by one man. I have spent twenty-seven years asking God why He was allowing one man to come against me like this and even though I still wait on God for an answer, there is always one truth that has never changed. God is here with me and He has never left me.

I could sit here and step by step tell you all the horrific and hurtful things that have played out through numerous civil offices and courts. I could walk you through every ugly thing but when it comes down at the end of the day no one needs to hear how evil tried to hurt me. Anyone looking for details of my divorce and custody trials, I am sorry to report to you, that you won't find them here. The details that transpired in my testimony here are an account of my feelings and hurts that God has helped bring me through. Evil is the absence of a relationship with God in your life. If you don't have God in your life and you're not living to serve Him then every ugly, hurtful thing you do represents His absence. That is all that I have to say about the evil that my ex has allowed into his life. Telling everyone my side of the story doesn't make or break my testimony. My valley was deep and my mountains were high, but my God was greater than them all. I am a living testimony that the lies, drama, and hurt did not break me. My God protected me, provided for me, and brought me through.

I have had people read this book and tell me that I needed to put more of the bad stuff that I went through in here so that people would know the mountain God had brought me through. I have weighed the measures and have prayed about doing that and God keeps telling me that no good can from digging back into those grave clothes. That doing so would only be for revenge or to hurt them back for the evil they had done to me. God tells me that the revenge is His and that I needed to lay all the hurt, pain, and worry at His Cross. So that is where I want to leave it. You should too.

1

Chapter One: Who Am I?

I would like to introduce myself. I am a nobody. I have no great title or claim in this life. I have no doctorate. No wealth of money. No grand mantle that I carry or achievements to call my own. I am a stay-at-home mom whose purpose in this life is to keep my home nice, clean, and tidy. According to others, my only purpose is for me to stay at home, heal, care for myself, and take care of my six-year-old daughter who has Down's Syndrome. Give me time to heal from five heart attacks and several stints placed in my heart. All they think I need to concentrate on is tending to her and being everything she needs me to be. She relies on me for everything. From turning on the TV, dressing her, and feeding her. I am to worry about nothing and worry more about me. That's not who I am. I have been in the workforce since I was fifteen years old and have never looked back.

When I was younger, I had these grand ideals in my mind that God had this great future ready for me to walk into. I just had to figure out where the key was hidden to open my door. I have spent my life seeking the answer to this question, Who am I?

I have been a cashier, a waitress, a nurse, a pharmacy technician. I have held many different titles. I have owned many different types of businesses and have had my hand in building greater, bigger businesses for other people. I have built websites, graphics, logos, and printed material for large companies to succeed. I have been the lowest person on the pole and I have been the person gaining all the profit. But no matter who I was it was never enough for me. It never paid me enough to be able to relax and be at peace. To feel secure in who I was. In my mind, I planned to work hard and get all I could from the world and at the ripe old age of thirty-five years old, I was going to retire and see the world with my loved ones. The harder I worked the harder the work became. The more money I made, the harder it was to keep. Till finally, I came to the conclusion that I was asking all the wrong questions and therefore getting all the wrong answers.

I have known the Lord my whole life. I accepted the Lord as my savior when I was very young and have sought after Him ever since. I feel I lived my life according to His will every day. I went to church. I served where I thought I was needed. I was led by the Holy Spirit and am daily guided by Him.

I met my ex-husband in 1996. I wish that I could say there were some good and bad times but the hurt and pain that came in the end when he decided to leave in 2008 took away any goodness that could've possibly remained. We had a two-year-old daughter together and it wasn't bad enough that he once said he'd never be like the guys in my past who were cheaters but he turned out to be worse than them all put together. He and his family put me through hell here on Earth. I have concluded that he and his family wanted the lies to be true because it was the only way that they could justify the ugliness they were manifesting. Hurts no human with a heart would ever inflict on someone they claimed to have once loved. Everything from breaking into our houses to put dead skunks to trying to say my relationship with God was me hearing voices to try and prove to the judge that I was crazy. Like, I said I have been through hell. I have lost more jobs because of their lies than I care to admit. All you had to do was mention one of our names downtown and someone would say that they heard about that case. It went on for so long that lawyers who were volunteering in the court's clerks' offices went on to be judges in our later cases who had remembered seeing our files come across their desks. It got to be so bad that I just wanted to crawl into a corner and die.

No matter what they were trying to label me as I stood my ground and held my faith in the Lord that He was going to bring my daughter, Taylor, home and that we would be okay. It's been fifteen years and I am still waiting on God to answer my prayers. I never questioned who I was and I never strayed from my path with the Lord despite the ugliness that came at me. Don't get me wrong I have spent more time secluded and in my prayer closet just to keep my sanity but with the help of God, I have maintained righteousness.

It was the answer to this question and the relationship that I have with the Lord that led me to my kitchen table eight years ago, crying out to God that my life had to have more purpose than doing and going through what I was going through in my life at the time. It was a hard day. I had just lost another job because of my ex-husband and his devious ways. I sat at the table questioning God as to why He would allow my ex to do these things to me. That if He loved me why wouldn't He protect me? Why would those employers believe such a horrible person's lies? God knew I needed a job. Why would He allow this to happen to me?

I sat alone at the table questioning the point of my life. Wondering if the feelings of worthiness and greatness were only lies placed in my head by the enemy not actually from the Lord. I sat there and cried and wrestled with my thoughts and questioned Him until He answered me. I sat in the darkness; in the quiet for hours before I heard anything. I watched as my neighbors came home from work. Moving along through their day. Hurrying along getting in the house to get dinner ready. The car's headlights passed by as I sat feeling more and more invisible as each second passed by.

Out of nowhere, the Holy Spirit spoke. He said to me, "Make Bread." Every Christian has a point in time where their relationship was wanting to know more about this God who saved us to actually knowing and hearing God's voice intervene in their situation on a more personal level. He begins to speak directly to your soul. However, He's been speaking to you all along. Calling you out of your sin, out of your bad ways, out of the ugly situations. Calling you towards His Light. Calling out HIS purpose for your life. Calling you to the good that He has for you and away from the darkness of the world. Looking back that was one of those moments for me. He saw me in my darkness and He reached in and pulled me out of the miry clay. Up until this moment, I feel like I knew of God, but here is where I began to know Him as my Lord. As my friend. As my compass.

We all have a place marked in our lives where our testimony and relationship with God turned real. A place where satan, our enemy, made his move for our very life and God denied him access to us. A place where God no longer was just words on a page but a real person speaking directly to us. Saving us from evil. Saving us from ourselves.

Everyone has a story. Every Christian has a testimony to share with others. This is the middle of my story and I feel like it was a difficult one. That I have fought with myself for years on how to convey what God was doing in my life without glorifying the evil that was done to me. But throughout this time, God was with me and protecting me. Telling me I was going to be okay.

"Make Bread!?!?" That's what He said to me. "Make Bread!" I thought to myself, "Is He serious?!?" How can the answer to all my questions about my life be for me to make bread? I thought it was crazy! My Mom made bread for our family while I was growing up. To me, it looked like the easiest thing in the world to make. How could my purpose in life be found in learning how to make bread? Looking back on the situation, my pride was ridiculous! I fought with God for over three months on this matter. I wasn't going to make bread. I screamed at Him. My purpose couldn't come from showing Him that I could make bread. That's all He ever said to me about the matter. No explanation. No direction. Nothing except make bread. Then silence. He never elaborated or gave specifics or any other details.

Regardless of how many times I asked for more explanation on the matter. He never said another word. Dead silence. As if to say, I already told you what you needed to do. I'm not going to tell you again. There was just silence.

So I had to come to a place of submission to His Will and I had decided I will just make the bread to be done with it. First time. Fail. Second time. Fail. The third time fails. It took me long hours of research, experiments, and frustration before I concluded that all God wanted was my attention. One time I even had my Mom standing right beside me doing every step with her own batch to teach me how to make bread. Same ingredients. Same yeast. Same water. Her batch came out perfect. Light and fluffy; Actually edible. My batch was dense, hard, and unable to be eaten. Trash. It was then she looked at me and said God must need your attention. Because I don't know what's wrong...It was then I humbly said, "Okay, God. What is it you need for me to know?" He then said, *"You have to learn about the ingredients."* It was then God began to reveal to me His heart and our purpose here on Earth.

Lesson One.

"Learning about The Flour."

2 Timothy 1:9–10

"For God saved us and called us to live a holy life. He did this, not because we deserved it, but because that was His plan from before the beginning of time—to show us his grace through Christ Jesus. And now He has made all of this plain to us by the appearing of Christ Jesus, our Savior."

It was at this time that God taught me about how He made us. About how He made me. About who His people are. What we're made of. The ingredients of who we are and who we are to become. He taught me these things while He is teaching me about all of the ingredients to make my bread recipe. Not just which ingredients were to be used but the actual quality and the purity of the ingredients for God to work with. As He taught me about each of the ingredients, He taught me about how to prepare, store, and use each of these ingredients. He taught me that every flour has a very specific characteristic that makes it that specific flour and gave it its specific purpose in a recipe. Its color, texture, and flavor were what made it different. Every detail in the life of the grain of wheat was what added specialized qualities to the end products. Even the very ground where the wheat grew gives each flour a specific flavor, purpose, and use. Some flours have natural sugars and flavor profiles that affect the way it is baked. Other flours are drier than others and need more oil to create a great flavor profile. There was so much to learn about the many different flours and how I could use them and in this teaching, I realized the similarities these characteristics had to the events in our lives and the purpose God has for us. You see, when you look at everything in your life as God wants you to see them then the perspective of the lesson changes. It's not just knowledge anymore. It's a tool in your work belt that you can use in your everyday life.

Just like each flour, each Christian is a different color, has a different past, and different experiences in their lives that will bring a different aspect of their final testimony to create the perfect incense unto the Lord. Each ingredient adds a different "flavor" to the story of our lives. Each story is a different testimony to the goodness, grace, mercy, and love of who God is for us to share with others. Every struggle we have been through brings a new meaning of who He is. As Christians, our lives are all a testimony of Him.

We are called to refine our story to a testimony that can be used to teach others. We are called by God to listen to Him through the trial. We are called to be still and be the example of goodness and light on this Earth. Like wheat grains, none of us are perfect after we have been harvested. We had to go through being harvested from the field, our seeds had to be shucked from the wheat stalk, our casing had to go through the threshing floor and then we had to be ground at the mill before we could even think about being used by Him! Our ingredients need to be purified before God can use us. We were called to be Holy.

Lesson 2:
"Learning about The Water."

My second lesson was about the purity of water. Although, this lesson wasn't too hard for me to understand God started to reveal to me the characteristics of the purity of our hearts. Like water, our hearts need to be pure in their intentions. God tells us as Christians we are to abstain from evil so that we can be pure water. Untainted by evil and its ways. But while God is teaching me about the purity of water for bread making God goes deeper in revealing to me His heart for His people. He began showing me how in so many ways unclean water is like the uncleanliness of our hearts. The water used for making bread needs to be pure and without added chemicals, rust, or bacteria so that it does not hurt the final recipe for the bread. Our intentions needed to be pure like the water used to make the bread.

It was during this time I had begun my food preparation training and learned how to keep food clean, healthy, and safe while in your care. Nothing is more eye-opening than learning about unclean water with bad bacteria and what it does to the human body once it is ingested. I don't need to go into gross details about the bacteria that can be in water but that is how our unpure thoughts and our unpure intentions can defile our hearts. Just a small amount of ugly bacteria in our water can contaminate everything we are doing. Not only in ourselves but the ugliness can spread into other's lives too. Wrecking their relationships and taking from them their joy and peace.

If God tells you to stay away from something then it's best to heed His warning. If you know alcohol or drugs are bad for you, then it's best to stay away from them. It's God's will for us to be holy and righteous. Let's not take part in anything that He wouldn't approve of. I believe that it is those sins that lead us away from God and make our souls starve for more living water. His presence cannot be filled or replaced by any human, any drink, or any drug. No matter how hard we try we will never be able to be with God and also be deep in our sins. That is why we are called to be Holy.

1 Peter 1:14-16: "As obedient children, do not conform to the evil desires you had when you lived in ignorance. But just as He who called you is holy, so be holy in all you do; for it is written: "Be holy, because I am holy."

The definition of holiness according to Oxford Languages is it means the state of being holy. "a life of holiness and total devotion to God."

Becoming Holy can only be achieved by having a relationship with the Lord.

John 4:14 tells us,
"Jesus answered, "Everyone who drinks this water will be thirsty again, but whoever drinks the water I give them will never thirst. Indeed, the water I give them will become in them a spring of water welling up to eternal life."

As I began this food training I came across the chapters in Leviticus where God's holy priests had to make preparations and check their appearance just to be able to safely enter the tent where the Ark was that housed the presence of God. The steps they had to perform to make themselves pure before they could go before the Lord, to be able to talk to Him and discern His will for His people was intense. The cleansing, the washing, the cutting of their hair, and the preparations that went into cleaning their clothes just to be before the Lord was unreal! Please go to **Leviticus 14** and allow God to show you these things.

Want to go deeper? Read **1 Peter 2: 1-25**

Lesson 3:
 "The Yeast"

Whew! The Yeast. This was a hard ingredient. I thought my bread recipe was failing because everyone I turned to help me with my problems with the bread said it sounded like I had dead yeast. There is so much to learn about yeast before you can even start to make bread. Science says this ingredient is the one that makes your bread rise up. But in my experience is that it takes a perfect combination of all the ingredients to allow the bread to rise up and grow. Without flour, water, salt, fat, and sugar...yeast will do nothing. But with them in perfect condition then we have the makings of a great bread recipe.

Let me share with you a little small baker's lesson in making bread. Exposure to extreme heat and air will kill the yeast. Too much or too little flour and you'll affect the reaction required for growth. Too much water and you'll affect the reaction required for growth. Too much or too little sugar and you'll affect the reaction required for growth. Do you hear what God is saying? All these ingredients are vital in making bread and allowing it to grow into the perfect bread. Any variation in these ingredients will affect its growth. Just like every moment in our life has affected who we are in the world. Any effect that the other ingredients may have on the yeast has then changed the yeast and it will change the whole batch of dough.

Galatians 5:7-10: "You were running a good race. Who cut in on you to keep you from obeying the truth? That kind of persuasion does not come from the one who calls you. "A little yeast works through the whole batch of dough." I am confident in the Lord that you will take no other view. The one who is throwing you into confusion, whoever that may be, will have to pay the penalty."

So true. You only need a little yeast to affect a whole batch of flour. Too much yeast and your bread will rise too quickly and won't give you time to shape the bread into its baking form. Not enough yeast and it will not rise at all. How many of our lives have had "too much of the wrong affection" thrown in when we were too young? Or not enough of the correct love at all while growing up that has affected our growth to our rise? But He also tells us that it is someone other than Him who is the author of the confusion and that there will be a penalty that they will pay. Love is the perfect ingredient that has to be given to make our batch rise correctly. It was God's Love that perfected us. So many times our love was affected in some form to cause our mixture to stray from the truth. So many things and people have caused the yeast in our recipe to react differently than the way that God intended our hearts to react. Make sure your heart is reacting the way God wants you to react.

Lesson 4:
"The Oil and the Salt"

Without the oil and the salt, your mixture is tasteless. Without oil and salt, no one will want to taste your bread. If they do try it, it will be quickly rejected. It won't taste good. As Christians, we are called to be the salt of the Earth. I truly believe in these instructions it is God's purpose to lead others to Him through our life as an example. We aren't instructed to hurt others with God's Word. We aren't told to belittle and hate others with God's word. We are told to take them to the side and to show them in private the error of their sins. Showing them how to be a Christian and to be Christ-like. To follow after God with all your heart and to lead and rise up others to do the same.

Matthew 5:13-16
"You are the salt of the earth. But if the salt loses its saltiness, how can it be made salty again? It is no longer good for anything, except to be thrown out and trampled underfoot. "You are the light of the world. A town built on a hill cannot be hidden."

"Neither do people light a lamp and put it under a bowl. Instead, they put it on its stand, and it gives light to everyone in the house. In the same way, let your light shine before others, that they may see your good deeds and glorify your Father in heaven."

* * *

God has given us many scriptures with references to God's anointing oil being used to purify, heal, anoint, and sanctify others of their problems. Only in Jesus' Name are we called to do the same. We are nothing without Christ. We can do nothing without Him there. We cannot be salt or light without Christ in our hearts. But if we do not purify our lives to glorify God, then when we are thrown into a bad situation are our hearts going to point others to God or will we be a stumbling block for another believer? Does everything we say and do taste good to others? Do our motives and intentions fulfill our purpose as Christians? Or do we leave others depressed, hurt, angry, or mad at God? Without God's Love to be our anointing oil and His Voice to be our salt we will never be able to lovingly bring people to see God for the great Lord and Savior that He truly is.

Lesson 5:
"Leave it Alone"

This lesson was hard to learn and even harder to maintain. When making bread you have to proof your yeast. You mix your water, sugar, and oil in the bowl then mix in your yeast. It is then the first step, where you find something else to do while God does His thing. This is where I struggled. Still to this day, I have trouble sitting still. The world says a woman has to be busier, active, working, tending to, handling her family, her man, her kids her house, her business...Just to be perfect in their eyes. But God says to be still and to give it to Him to handle. For all the things we struggle with daily, Christ says to lay them all at His feet to be dealt with. He says to be at peace and to rest in the shadow of His wings.

Now I truly don't think that God is telling us not to go to work. Or to let our house go and let it become dirty because He will clean it for us.

God tells us in many scriptures that idle hands bring a fool into poverty. So let us be sure to be about the Lord's work. Make sure our homes are clean and tidy. Make sure our cars are presentable and clean. Make sure our laundry is folded and pressed. Everything we do is a reflection of God the Father to nonbelievers. Let us not give them a reason to not want to know Christ.

In all my baking lessons and what I have learned about life from God is to step back and stop touching the dough mixture. The more you touch the dough the more you aggravate it and dry it out. I feel like God was telling me to stop touching the situation. The more I allowed my flesh to be in the chaos the more it made things worse. So we need to stop arguing with the enemy. Stop giving the person room to argue. Stop aggravating the situation. Stop pushing their buttons. Stop allowing others to hurt you. Stop going there to that business that makes you uncomfortable. Stop listening to the negativity. Stop turning to that channel. Stop going to that website. Just Stop! Just be still. When applied to baking bread it is the perfect answer. Mix the ingredients. Form the dough. Leave it alone.

I believe that the same lesson can be applied to our lives. God creates us. He allows life to mix in its special ingredients. Then He forms us and then in His presence, He allows us to rise. He blesses us with direction and with His favor and then He allows us to rise up; to become an example to the world. It is in this rising time that I feel like God decides on whether or not we are ready to be placed in the oven, or into the fire. You see, until we are perfectly formed we can't be placed in the oven. The fire in the oven sets us on our course to live out His testimony and share the gospel with others. If we don't have all the correct ingredients in our mixture then we won't be useful and effective in the fire. The fire will be the test of whether we can listen to everything God has taught us. Because in the fire is when we will truly be tested. In the fire, we will see whether we can hold up to HIS golden standards. In the fire, we should shine in His glory.

Once we have been placed in the oven we will be set firmly on our path. Our form will be permanent. Will we meet God's standards? Or will we be dense and unable to be used at God's ability? Will our testimony be edible so that others can learn and glean from our trials? Or are we still bitter, too salty, and thick to be eaten? Or do we need to be reformed? Reconstructed so that when placed in the fire we will rise up light and fluffy. Ready to be used? Ready to be harnessed with

God's sweet confections?

Isaiah 20:30: "And though the Lord give you the bread of adversity and the water of affliction, yet your Teacher will not hide Himself any more, but your eyes shall see your Teacher."

It was after these lessons that my business came into existence. It was called All Things Edible. I opened a company that made homemade fresh breads, pies, cinnamon rolls, cookies cheesecakes…All Things Edible. We catered food for events for companies and individuals. We started baking out of my home and before too long we had a storefront in town. We opened right before Covid hit and were doing okay until God decided to redirect my plans for the future. But all things are possible with God. You can always be sure that if God is telling you to do something the door will fling wide open and He will provide everything you need to do what HE wants you to do. I thought that my lifelong search for His Purpose was finally over. Everything I had learned in my life was learned because I was going to own this business and was going to do great things in my community.

I planned to own my company, have some employees I could train to do what I needed them to do, be successful, and never have to worry about anything again. I'm sure you've heard the ole' saying "Want to see God laugh? Tell Him what your plans are for your future!" God always has a better plan for our lives than we do. We may not know it but He is always trying to get us to surrender ugly things; sin, regret, fear, doubt, anger, hate, jealousy, rage, our broken hearts. He is always telling us to give those things to Him. He wants to free our hearts. Show us a better way of living.

Now don't get me wrong we can become comfortable with these things. Right? We have lived with the hurt for so long, that we don't know how to live without it. It's almost like satan has Stockholm syndromed us into a life of bondage. We hold onto these hurtful things like our lives depend on them. We tell God we can't do it when He never asked us to do anything. All He is saying is Let it go. So when the Holy Spirit comes in and asks us to be someone God has called us to be, we feel somewhat scared maybe even violated. Because we have held on to those identities that satan built for us instead of clinging to God's word and defining our lives the way God sees us.

1 John 3:1-3

"See what great love the Father has lavished on us, that we should be called children of God! And that is what we are! The reason the world does not know us is that it did not know Him. Dear friends, now we are children of God, and what we will be has not yet been made known. But we know that when Christ appears, we shall be like Him, for we shall see Him as He is. All who have this hope in Him purify themselves, just as He is pure."

I feel that is why so many people get so angry towards Christians. Once we have our worldly sunglasses taken off and we see the world for what it truly is and we learn who we are in God's true opinion we begin to want to share that great news with others. We want others to see that they are living a depressed life but they don't have to. We want them to see that love that we see and feel in God is there for everyone to have. Others feel that God wants them to let go of everything they think they are but what they don't realize is that He has a better plan for them. A life that is free of shame, hurt, pain, sin, and anger. He wants everyone to come home and be with Him in the garden again. God wants to be with us. He loves us. He wants us to know Him better. He wants us to know the truth and to believe in Him. But to get closer to Him we have to get rid of the unholy things from our lives. He cannot partner with the things that are hurting us so badly. He is telling us there is a better way.

So in Sept when I had five heart attacks and God was telling me that I had to close my store, I was not too happy. That was putting it nicely. I will be honest. I was kicking and screaming; bartering with God to let me keep the life that I had built for myself. I fought Him so hard on the matter that He took my health completely away from me. I couldn't walk without having chest pains and shortness of breath for any more than five feet. I couldn't move, hardly talk, and taking care of my daughter was a serious chore for me. I became bitter, angry, and mad. I couldn't understand why this was happening to me after I had come so far from the kitchen table when He asked me to make bread. I kept asking the doctors why wasn't I getting better. They ran their tests. Everything came back that I was okay. There was no reason why I shouldn't be breathing better and be able to walk. I was on medicines that were supposed to help heal my heart but the daily simple chores of life were still really hard. Churches all around me were praying for me and speaking into my life. Still, my health wasn't getting any better.

Finally, in February, I could no longer keep putting things off. The building owner asked me to have all my equipment out of the space we rented. In frustration, I asked God how this miraculous task was going to happen under such short notice. Praying for a miracle He answered and told me that He was going to sell it all in two days. I began crying because I knew when the Holy Spirit speaks then you get immediate confirmation in your spirit. I knew it was going to happen. I told my husband, Paul, what the Holy Spirit said and he told me he didn't see how it was going to happen either and that we would look into other feasible answers. Two days later almost everything was gone. When God says He's going to do something He doesn't give you time to doubt Him. He just does it. All Things Edible was now closed and I found myself back at the table crying out to God again. "God, what are your plans now? Now that I am disabled and unable to go to work. Now that I have a kid that needs me to care for her." Here I am again without a purpose and a meaning for my life. Here I was again down on my knees. If God had allowed these changes to take place in my life and I wasn't going to be a business owner and a baker, then I was asking the wrong question. Instead of asking, "Who am I?" I found myself asking a different question this time and hoping to find the correct answer.

"Who am I to God?"

In this chapter, I spoke on Who I thought I was. Every person has a description of who they believe they are to other people. So tell me here who or what defines you. Does your career? Does your family? Does your church? Do you label yourself a mother, a baker, an aunt, or a sister? Tell me who you think you are…

_____

_____

_____

_____

_____

_____

_____

_____

_____

_____

Now read this prayer with me:

Dear Lord,

My name is _____. I want to be a better version of myself for you. Help me to see myself through your eyes. Help me to find more of you in my day. Give me the courage to speak your truth and your will to my heart. Help me to realize your ways are not my ways and that my thoughts are not your thoughts. Give me your peace and allow your ways and thoughts to become my own. In Jesus' mighty name. Amen

"See what kind of love the Father has given to us, that we should be called children of God; and so we are. The reason why the world does not know us is that it did not know Him." ~1 John 3:1

2

Chapter 2: Who Am I to God?

Deep down in the depths of my soul, I know how to answer this question. I can spit off quotes and scriptures that my mind tells me is true. As a Christian, I know all the right answers but if I am being honest with you, I don't feel the words as truth in my life. I heard it once said in my psychology class in college that for every ugly or bad phrase spoken over life, it takes seven good phrases to cancel the word of negativity. People speak to others as if they don't care how it affects them. With such freedom from any consequences. Look on social media platforms, people speak their thoughts before thinking of the consequences of what they're speaking. Would they be so free to act in such an ugly way if they were face to face with an actual person? People have taken the Freedom of Speech to a whole new level. A hurtful level.

It's not just the secular world acting this way. It is Christians as well. It's like people forget that they are talking to a human being with feelings, a mind, a soul, a heart, and a memory. Children talk to adults; to their parents in the most demeaning and hurtful ways. Young adults use bad language and carry on in the workplace like they were raised by crazy people who didn't know how to act. It's like when we got rid of God in our schools and out of our lives we forgot all His great advice on how to live. Everything that God taught you was thrown out the window and dismissed as offensive. It's almost as if being Godly wasn't accepted as the truth in our life. It's almost like there is someone out there trying to prove God is not God. Well, there is someone out there like that. It started with the rebellion of satan and his followers being kicked out of heaven for their disobedience. Ever since then satan has done nothing but try and prove that God is not our true living good God that He is. He first appeared in the Garden of Eden and he will not stop until Christ's return spoken in Revelations. However, God tells us that we are responsible for our speech.

Proverbs 18:20-21

"From the fruit of their mouth, a person's stomach is filled; with the harvest of their lips, they are satisfied. The tongue has the power of life and death, and those who love it will eat its fruit."

James 1:19-26

"My dear brothers and sisters, take note of this: Everyone should be quick to listen, slow to speak, and slow to become angry because human anger does not produce the righteousness that God desires.

Therefore, get rid of all moral filth and the evil that is so prevalent and humbly accept the word planted in you, which can save you. Do not merely listen to the word, and so deceive yourselves. Do what it says.

Anyone who listens to the word but does not do what it says is like someone who looks at his face in a mirror and, after looking at himself, goes away and immediately forgets what he looks like. But whoever looks intently into the perfect law that gives freedom, and continues in it—not forgetting what they have heard, but doing it—they will be blessed in what they do.

Those who consider themselves religious and yet do not keep a tight rein on their tongues deceive themselves, and their religion is worthless."

The pain this world causes us is horrifying. The murders, the stealing, the raping, the lying...and I'm just referencing what newsworthy advertised ways that people are hurting each other. If you watch the internet news or social media, the actions and the pain can be so damaging it would take a miracle from God to heal from it.

Don't get me started on the hurt and pain that can be caused by the courts in a divorce or a child custody dispute.

I understand the hurt others can cause someone. Maybe not the way some do but I understand that we all have been hurt. One way or another. We see each day coming with such fear and resentment that I seriously don't know how people live without the love and direction of Christ. I have had some of the worst things done to me and yet I know some have had worse. I have been called every bad word in the book. The enemy on occasion has even tried to label me as things that I am clearly not. Your enemy is a slanderous, manipulative, low down dirty player. He will stop at nothing to steal from you. He will try to steal or use your children, your grandchildren, your friends, family, and loved ones. He will steal your job, your car, your house, your vacation home. His plans are to kill you in ten different ways and will stop at nothing to destroy your life, your reputation, and your livelihood. I have experienced it; firsthand. So I know what you might be going through.

If I may, can I recommend some other wonderful books that have helped me understand these things through my journey. Aside from the Bible. These books work and talk about life following the Bible. The first book helped me when I was in the thick of an attack. The author is a world-renowned pastor and author. His name is Dr. Charles Stanley. Before I could finish writing this book, he has since left us to be with the Lord. I will never forget how his ministry has supported me and touched my life. I will be forever grateful to him for his obedient walk with the Lord. The book he wrote is called ***When the Enemy Strikes.*** The Holy Spirit gave me this book when I needed a better perspective during my horrific divorce. I won't go into the evil that was portrayed against me because I am not writing this book to glorify evil. I want to glorify God. Let's just say it helped me understand the battles I was facing and it helped me keep my head and eyes on the Lord. Partnered with scripture it calls out many of the evils that come against us every day.

The second book is written by Joyce Meyer. Called ***The Battlefield of the Mind.*** The enemy can attack our physical realm but his biggest playground is when we allow him into our thoughts. We allow him to terrorize our thought processes and ultimately our decisions. He uses whatever demonic rulers he can to take us out. We cannot control what other people do, but we can control our thoughts and our own reactions to any situation. There are many examples of people in the Bible who were attacked and assaulted, but I want you to take a look at King David. He tells us throughout the *Book of Psalms* how he was tormented and how he knew his enemies were out to kill him. In his writings, we see his biggest struggle was the thoughts he had to take captive every day. He had to keep fear, anxiety, self-doubt, depression, sexual immorality, and disobedience out of his heart and mind.

Back to the point in my story...Once all the equipment and the store front were gone I was left with a great sadness and a deep depression. Did I do something wrong? Did I not hear God correctly? Did I tithe enough? What did I do to allow God to take such drastic measures? As I thought about the words that were crossing my mind and heart, I remembered God does not cause us harm. He tells us that His thoughts for us are more than the sands in the seas. That He has every hair on my head numbered. So why in the world would He cause me harm if He loves me so? It was time for me to go back into the Word and find out exactly who I am to God. I had to see it for myself. I had to read with my very eyes how God feels about me. Once I found out the answer to that question, then I felt I would be able to move forward to what I needed to do and who I needed to be. I would be able to move forward and move on with my life.

Well okay. I went to the Bible to find the answer and found my scriptures for me to stand on. Then I Googled the question "Who does God say I am?" I found many scriptures of who God says that I am. When I accepted the Lord Jesus Christ as my Lord and Savior, I found out that I am a new creature. I have been saved since I was seven years old and I still sometimes forget that I am not what the world says that I am. God is real. He sent His only son to die on the cross for my sins and that can never be taken away from me. Nothing can take God's love for me away. The Bible tells me that God's thoughts for me are more than the sands that are in the seas! Here are just a few of His revelations.

I am Saved: 2 Timothy 1:9: "Who has saved us and called *us* with a Holy calling, not according to our works, but according to His purpose and grace which was given to us in Christ

Jesus before time began." Through the sacrifice of Jesus' blood on the cross I am saved from my sins. My past sins, my current sins, and my future sins. Any crimes that I have ever committed against God the Father have been wiped from the Book of Life. He keeps no records of any of my wrongs. If you have any sins against the Father all God tells us that all we need to do is repent of those sins. In plain terms, we just need to ask God to forgive us for those sins. That's it. It is gone. It is finished. They are no longer there. The sins written on the pages of my life will disappear and my pages are again white as snow. I always see them rising off the page like chalk dust blowing in the wind. Disappearing like they were never there.

Now that my sins have been forgiven there is something you need to know. Your sins are forgiven by the Father God but that doesn't always mean that the hurt you caused a loved one is gone. It is still there and now it is time to make those wrongs right again. The money that you stole must be returned. The hateful things you spoke about a coworker must be apologized for. There are many ways to say you are sorry but the most important one is the one that comes from the heart.

That isn't always an easy task. Asking someone that we hurt to forgive us for our actions. They won't always see things your way. They sometimes have their own demons that they are dealing with. You can't control how they react, but you can control how you move forward. God always tells us to move forward in love. So we take the apology to them and pray that it is righted in their hearts but you might have to follow through with more love and actions to prove that you're worthy of their forgiveness. Prove to them that your apology is truthful. It might take a while. That's okay. Keep Moving Forward. Maintain Godly righteousness at all costs. Maintain Holiness regardless of what their reaction may be. The hurt you caused may warrant their strong defensive measures to come into place. If you value them in your life then you will have to stick it out and allow them to see the work that God is doing in your life. Allow them to see the transformation that has caused such a radical change in your behavior. Let them see the fruits of the love of God working in your heart. It'll be worth it. Prayerfully, in the end, both of your lives with be forever changed and your hearts will be healed.

~*~

I am Chosen: 1 Thessalonians 1:4: "We know, dear brothers and sisters, that God loves you and has chosen you to be His own people." Since He first knit me in my mother's womb He marked me and has chosen me to be forever His. I am His daughter. I am His princess. I am His Chosen. There is such a burden of relief once you realize that you have been chosen. That you're not just here to be here. That God has chosen you to be on His team. Remember back in the day when you were young and you were getting ready to play ball in the neighborhood with all your friends. Teams were being picked and the third round of friends had been picked to be on the best team and there were only a few of you left. So you still hadn't been picked out of the group. Your self-esteem was getting low. Every horrible thought runs through your head. I am not good enough. I am not a good runner, a good hitter, a good catcher. I don't slide that well. I don't hit home runs. I don't do whatever it is that should get me picked…But then you finally have a team and you still don't feel worthy or good enough. Many of us have allowed that burden of worthiness to carry into our adult lives. Something horrible happened to change your perception of yourselves and you can't move past the label that you aren't good enough for the team. The good team. The best team. So every decision is made thinking you aren't good enough to get what you want out of your life.

Maybe your father left your mother and you thought it was because of something you did. So the shame has followed you most of your life. Maybe your grandparent labeled you as an evil kid and you took it to heart and began acting out more. Maybe you were homeless and you had to sell your body for food to eat. Maybe you started taking pills because of a work injury and got addicted. Maybe you wanted to not feel the ugliness of the world anymore and you numbed the hurt out with alcohol. Whatever it was that scarred your life with these hurtful things, God says that is not who you are. That those sins are not the things that identify who you are. From the time of your acceptance of the Lord into your life, you became a new person. You were chosen to be on HIS TEAM. The gifts that God has given you are the gifts that should define you. Like with all teams you have a new uniform you must wear. Being on God's team you have to maintain the purity, holiness, righteousness, and goodness. Being chosen means you have to be done with your old ways. God is asking you to trust Him with that hurt and pain that caused you to run to the hurtful things in your life. To take that uniform that He is giving you and walk out on that field with the authority to handle your business. Let Him deal with all the hurt and shame. Walk with His Glory upon your face.

You don't want to hold on to those hurtful things anyways, do you? No, you want to move forward to a future of being whole again. With God's help, all things are possible. Breaking all those chains of bondage is possible. Tearing down the walls that are keeping you from happiness is gone. Anxiety, fear, pain, hurt…all gone from your life. You are Chosen.

John 15:16 says,

"You did not choose me, but I chose you and appointed you that you should go and bear fruit and that your fruit should abide, so that whatever you ask the Father in my name, He may give it to you."

~*~

I am Forgiven:

1 John 2:12: "I write to you, little children Because your sins are forgiven you for His name's sake." No matter what you have done. God says that because of Jesus Christ's sacrifice on the cross, we are forgiven for our transgressions. Our sins are no longer there. They have been wiped away. When we accepted Jesus Christ into our hearts and we repented for our sins, God says, "You are forgiven. Go and sin no more."

Go and sin no more. That means we don't go back and do the things that He has forgiven us for. If He forgave you for stealing that means you are no longer a thief. That means we have to retrain your mind and body to not want to do those things again. If you stole to live and buy bread then you have to find another way to get money to buy the bread. There are many sins we are accustomed to using and each one of them is going to take strength and God's help to overcome. It may even take a few good friends who have your best interests at heart to help you. Don't be afraid to ask someone to help you overcome your fears and your sins. As a matter of fact, I think it should be something you should do. Having someone help hold you accountable and can encourage you till you can learn to overcome them on your own. I have seen failure happen so many times. Yes, God forgives us and He can help give us strength in our weakest times but a true

Christian friend will help hold you up when the enemy attacks your mind. Trust me, he will come to attack you. If you are trying to live right and live for God, satan and his minions hate nothing more. He sends every attack he can to keep you from that goal. All of a sudden you'll see more ads for the very things you are trying to stay away from. An alcoholic will see more ads selling beer or liquor. A drug addict will see more dealers on corners where they live. Sex addicts will see more trash than they ever saw living in sin. So when those attacks come and they seem to be unbearable then having that friend(s) to help you stay on your path is the loaded weapon you need against the enemy. Especially if it is a Christian friend who knows the Word of God to use against the enemy.

Choose someone who is not of the opposite sex. Men; find male friends. Females; find female supporters. People who can keep you away from your problem areas and keep you on your goals to live for Christ. Trust me, you don't want new problems in your life by falling into another bad situation that you'll need more help with later. Meet in public places. A coffee shop or a food court. By staying in public areas everyone tends to remain pure and on task. When people get comfortable things tend to go astray. Remember, the goal is to keep you away from your addictions and to encourage you in the lifestyle God has and wants for you. Make sure everything that is spoken to you aligns with the Word of God. If your support help is telling you something contrary to God's Word then you need to find a new support person.

Philippians 4:8-9: "Finally, brethren, whatever things are true, whatever things *are* noble, whatever things *are* just, whatever things *are* pure, whatever things *are* lovely, whatever things *are* of good report, if *there is* any virtue and if *there is* anything praiseworthy—meditate on these things. The things which you learned and received and heard and saw in me, these do, and the God of peace will be with you."

Once we have come to a place where God is healing us we won't want to go back to our old ways. So our bodies and minds won't concentrate on the things that will hurt us. We will begin to think about the things that God wants us to think about. Our Future!

On the good things again. In Him!

~*~

I am Created for Good Works:

Ephesians 2:10: "For we are His workmanship, created in Christ Jesus for good works, which God prepared beforehand, that we should walk in them." Read that again, because I don't think you understood that. You were created to do good work. You were created to do good things in this life. You were not created to hurt others. You were not created to plot evil in the night. You were not created to steal, kill, or destroy. You were created to be good. Because of the horrible situations that you have had to live through, some of us tend to think that we weren't made for good things. I'm sorry that you believe that because it's a lie straight from hell. You were not created to do evil. No one was. No one was born on this Earth to hurt others. It might be easier for you to hurt others. Your situations might have trained your mind to see the bad easier than the good but that's not why God made you. Believe me, HE MADE YOU. You were not created in a petri dish. You are not made of plastic or wood. God breathed your first breath into your life and you came to be.

God is the only Living God who controls the universe. He is omnipotent, all-knowing, a living, breathing God. Regardless of the people or the situation that brought you into this time, it was still God that sparked the life into you. God saw you in His mind and created you in the spark of your mother's womb.

Colossians 1:6: "For by Him all things were created, in heaven and on earth, visible and invisible, whether thrones or dominions or rulers or authorities—all things were created through Him and for Him."

We were created for Him by Him to do His good works. We were created to praise Him. Glorify Him. Love Him. He saw you and had a purpose for your life. He has plans for you. **Jeremiah 29:11,** God tells us, **"For I know the plans I have for you," declares the LORD, "plans to prosper you and not to harm you, plans to give you hope and a future."**

So let's talk this part out. If God's plans for us are for good, then why is there so much bad running around in this world?

Why are there so many bad things happening to us? Why are people being so mean to me? Hurting me? Hurting the ones I love? Why did my husband cheat on me and ruin us? Why did that guy rape me and beat me? Why does my boyfriend drink so much that he hurts my feelings? Why did my wife take my son from me and marry another man? Why did my parents let that uncle touch me like that? Why did my kid steal money from me to buy drugs out on the street?

If God loves us so much why does HE allow such hurt to happen in this world? I asked my brother one time why he fought to go to church and love the Lord so hard. I couldn't believe his answer. He is a military man and has seen the world and a lot of the hurt in it. He said, "I have seen too much bad. How could there be a God who would allow so much hurt and death to happen?" I have pondered his answer to the question for many years. Why does God allow it to happen? To Christians and non-believers alike. There is so much hurt and pain. Destruction. For my answers, I always have to go to the Bible. I have to hear from Him why these things are happening. He tells us why. He shows us why. He gives us examples of the why. He lays it all out for us in ways only we as Christians can understand.

It is because He has given us free will. He gives us free will to choose Him. He gives us the choice to love Him. Think of it like this. Parents, you train your child to listen and obey. You tell them where their shoes go when they come inside the house. Do you like to have to tell them every time to take their shoes off and put them away? Over and over again? They keep having to be told to take their shoes off and not to run through the house with dirty shoes on. No, you want them to be told once and they willingly listen to you and obey. They choose to love you and want to spend time with you and do as they should. You want their wants to be the same as your wants. Free will.

Revelations 3:20 "Here I am! I stand at the door and knock. If anyone hears my voice and opens the door, I will come in and eat with that person, and they with me."

Joshua 24:15 "And if it is evil in your eyes to serve the LORD, choose this day whom you will serve, whether the gods your fathers served in the region beyond the river; or the gods of the Amorites in whose land you dwell. But as for me and my house, we

will serve the LORD."

John 1:12-13   "But to all who did receive Him, who believed in His name, He gave the right to become children of God, who were born, not of blood nor of the will of the flesh nor of the will of man, but of God."

We were given the choice to choose to be good over evil. We can choose to help others or leave them hurt. We can choose to feed the homeless or we can leave them to starve. We can choose to give our coats to those who are cold or we can let them freeze. All people were created and given the ability to choose God's love. We pray for God to heal the broken, feed the poor, and give shelter to the homeless. Why can't we be God's answer to those who are hurting? We were given the gift to choose life. We can choose to live life by the Spirit of the Lord or to live life through evil. We can choose to quietly talk and understand or we can quickly judge them and be loud in public. We can choose to love instead of hate.

Galatians 5:13-26:
" You, my brothers and sisters, were called to be free. But do not use your freedom to indulge the flesh; rather, serve one another humbly in love.

14 For the entire law is fulfilled in keeping this one command: "Love your neighbor as yourself."

15 If you bite and devour each other, watch out or you will be destroyed by each other.

16 So I say, walk by the Spirit, and you will not gratify the desires of the flesh.

17 For the flesh desires what is contrary to the Spirit, and the Spirit what is contrary to the flesh. They are in conflict with each other; so that you are not to do whatever you want.

18 But if you are led by the Spirit, you are not under the law.

19 The acts of the flesh are obvious: sexual immorality, impurity, and debauchery;

20 idolatry and witchcraft; hatred, discord, jealousy, fits of rage, selfish ambition, dissensions, factions

21 and envy; drunkenness, orgies, and the like. I warn you, as I did

before, that those who live like this will not inherit the kingdom of God.

22 But the fruit of the Spirit is love, joy, peace, forbearance, kindness, goodness, faithfulness,

23 gentleness and self-control. Against such things, there is no law.

24 Those who belong to Christ Jesus have crucified the flesh with its passions and desires.

25 Since we live by the Spirit, let us keep in step with the Spirit.

26 Let us not become conceited, provoking, and envying each other.

I love how this scripture tells us to live life in step with the Spirit. For those of you who don't know, the Spirit that is being referenced is the Holy Spirit. When Christ died on the cross and rose from the dead He tells us that the Spirit would come to be with us and to guide us in His absence. (**Refer to Acts 2.**) Once we are saved and we have given our life to Christ, we are called to be Christ-like. Hence the name Christians. Living by the guidance of the Holy Spirit we are called to produce good actions. Actions that produce joy, peace, forbearance, kindness, goodness, faithfulness, gentleness, self-control, and LOVE. Everything we do. Every action. Every word. Every sound is supposed to produce these good qualities and characteristics. Every sentence we speak to another human being is supposed to bring loving, kind, peace, joy... EVERY ONE of them is supposed to invoke a feeling of goodness. Not evil.

Ephesians 4:29, "Let no corrupting talk come out of your mouths, but only such as is good for building up, as fits the occasion, that it may give grace to those who hear."

Ephesians 5:11: "Take no part in the unfruitful works of darkness, but instead expose them."

Proverbs 11:12: "Whoever belittles his neighbor lacks sense, but a man of understanding remains silent."

But we're are called to produce love? That's a hard one. We are supposed to love everyone. We are supposed to love them regardless of their religious affiliation.We are supposed to love them regardless of their political views. We are supposed to love them regardless of their drug addictions. We may not love their sins, but we are called to love them to Christ. We are called to show them the way to love. We are called to show them grace, mercy, peace, and love as it is manifested in our own lives. The relationship we have with the Father is the only way we can produce those characteristics in our life for someone else. If we try to help someone without the love and guidance from the Father then we do it in vain. For if we aren't leading them to Him then nothing we do will ever work. That's why we are called to go to our secret place and spend so much time in prayer with God because He is the only one who can show us how to love the hardest people. He is the only one who can tell us how to lead an unbeliever to Him. He is the only one who can show us how to speak to the hurting, fearful, angry, and tormented. In our ways, we are unable to show the love of Christ. Through Him, we can do HIS WILL for our lives. In Him, we can LOVE them all.

In this chapter I learned about Who I am to God. After spending time in your secret place with the Lord and in His scriptures, what has He revealed to your heart about Who you are to Him?

_____

_____

_____

_____

_____

_____

_____

_____

Also, has He revealed the lies that the enemy has spoken over your life and told you Who you are NOT? Please write these revelations down here. When we journal what God has revealed to us as truths, it is important to write them down so that we can reflect on them later when the enemy tries to use those same lies again.

_____

_____

_____

_____

_____

_____

_____

_____

_____

Now pray this prayer with me:

Dear Lord,

I am a child of God. I am yours. By accepting Jesus Christ as my Lord and Savior, I am now your daughter/son. I am saved. I am chosen. I am forgiven. I am loved. Help me to accept these truths in my heart and help me to feel them in my soul. Help me to carry myself as your child and give me the courage to come against the lies the enemy may want to come against me with. Help me to rebuke the lies of the enemy with the voice YOU have given me. God, walk with me in the days ahead and put others in my life that can help support your thoughts of me in my reality. In Jesus' mighty name. Amen.

"For we are his workmanship, created in Christ Jesus for good works, which God prepared beforehand, that we should walk in them." ~Ephesians 2:10

3

Chapter 3: Love Honestly

God, we aren't supposed to love them all right? We don't have to love everyone, right? I don't have to love the girl in my high school chemistry class that stole my boyfriend, right? We don't have to love our controlling, micromanaging dictator of a boss, right? I don't have to love the man who took my daughter and poisoned her against me, right? Right?

God, you don't understand what they did. You don't understand what they took from me. You don't know how they made me feel. God, you just don't understand. Because if you did understand then you would never ask me to love them. They don't have any good in them. They've done evil things. They don't want good for me. Why should I want good for them? They don't have any light in them at all. So why do I have to share my light with them? They don't deserve my love. They are not worthy of my love. Why would you ask me to do such a thing? How does my love help them? How does it help you, God? How does my loving my enemy help me? How does my love help me get over this hurt? The pain? The fear? The anxiety that person has caused me?

We can ponder these questions for eternity. The whats, the wheres, the hows, but the answers will never be enough. They only lead to more questions that go unanswered. More frustration and a sense of feeling abandoned. So that all is left to do is to go over and over in your mind what and where you went wrong. I found myself at the end of this pathway. The tunnel felt dark, lonely, and cold. I felt alone. I came to a place where it only brought me more pain. A place where the loss seemed to be unbearable. I felt broken. I felt like I was unable to be fixed. I had lost all my hope.

It was then I was taken to a scripture that changed everything. I knew in my heart and mind that God always had given me the right scriptures to understand what I was going through, so why wouldn't they now? If we are supposed to love a world that is nothing like us because of Jesus Christ then it is up to us to go to Jesus Christ to find out how we are supposed to finish our task in loving them correctly. Like He would.

1 John 3:1-3: "See what great love the Father has lavished on us, that we should be called children of God! And that is what we are! The reason the world does not know us is that it did not know him. Dear friends, now we are children of God, and what we will be has not yet been made known. But we know that when Christ appears, we shall be like Him, for we shall see Him as He is. All who have this hope in Him purify themselves, just as He is pure."

I looked at the books of the Bible and I had never read **2 Corinthians**. So I opened it up and started reading. I had no indication that it would lead me as it did. I had no pastor preaching a sermon on what I wanted to know. I just trusted my heart and let my heart and soul guide me. **2 Corinthians** had the revelation that put me in the right frame of mind to move forward.

" If anyone has caused grief, he has not so much grieved me as he has grieved all of you to some extent—not to put it too severely. The punishment inflicted on him by the majority is sufficient. Now instead, you ought to forgive and comfort him, so that he will not be overwhelmed by excessive sorrow. I urge you, therefore, to reaffirm your love for him. Another reason I wrote you was to see if you would stand the test and be obedient in everything. Anyone you forgive, I also forgive. And what I have forgiven—if there was anything to forgive—I have forgiven in the sight of Christ for your sake, in order that Satan might not outwit us. For we are not unaware of his schemes.

* * *

Now when I went to Troas to preach the gospel of Christ and found that the Lord had opened a door for me, I still had no peace of mind, because I did not find my brother Titus there. So I said goodbye to them and went on to Macedonia.

But thanks be to God, who always leads us as captives in Christ's triumphal procession and uses us to spread the aroma of the knowledge of him everywhere. For we are to God the pleasing aroma of Christ among those who are being saved and those who are perishing. To the one we are an aroma that brings death; to the other, an aroma that brings life. And who is equal to such a task? Unlike so many, we do not peddle the word of God for profit. On the contrary, in Christ, we speak before God with sincerity, as those sent from God."

Those are some tough questions, aren't they? If we can't understand the why, the how, and the purpose of God's plan then we truly can't get behind it. We can't understand all the intricate details of God's will for our lives. Here in scripture, we can. God calls us to forgive others because WE WERE FORGIVEN. To withstand the test and be obedient to the Father. To be obedient because we were sent to tell others about His Light and to tell the world. It is through us that they might get to know Him!

So how are we supposed to share God's Light with the world? Love them. When they hit us; Love them. When they cheat on us; Love them. When they steal from us; Love them. But how are we supposed to do that when every fiber in our body says we are to lash out in a hurtful way? When our friends say we should do something to retaliate. Our bodies and minds are created from the experiences of our past. When we disobeyed our parents when we were young it laid the foundation of our understanding of our future. We did something wrong we got spanked. We disobeyed their rules we got punished. We acted out and disrespected them we got something taken away from us. Bad behavior or actions always invoked bad consequences. That can be said for the opposite as well. When we did something good we got praised. We got showed off. We got hugs and love. We got rewarded for the good we did. Don't read this the wrong way. I am not giving an opinion on disciplining your kids. God tells us that if we spare the rod then we spoil the child. But that is a discussion for another book. I am just pointing out that we are a manifestation of how our experiences have shaped us to be.

When we look at the world the way the world raised us and trained us to see things then it is only plausible that we would understand when we see it work in our lives. Others are treating us badly so we have to retaliate in the same form. When we get punched then we have to punch back. We are screamed at then we have to scream at them. If our boss doesn't see our hard work then there is no reason to work hard. Or maybe even worse the world has trained us that people's bad and hurtful actions towards us mean they are not worthy of our love and we should cut them out of our lives...We should let them go and let someone else deal with them.

This was a hard concept for me to understand. I guess it comes from having a disconnected father during my childhood. But I could never understand how it would be better for the family member to be sent away than to be with their loving family. I have read many fiction books and fiction tales of people sending their kids away because of the problems they had caused in the home. I could never understand how loving them from afar was better for anyone. It wasn't until we took in my husband's sister's boy into our home and had to be responsible for him that I realized there was nothing more that I could do for him and we had to give him back to the courts. His inability to listen to anything we said, the drugs he was getting from his family at visits, and his running away were so disruptive that we couldn't even go to work. This child needed constant "knee on his neck" attention that was just intolerable. This was a child you could see in his eyes when God was working in him and when He wasn't. It wasn't till I started to fear the road he was on was more than we could bare that we knew enough was enough.

Now don't go and get all upset with me. There are some harmful situations that you and your family should not endure for love. If someone is abusing you or your children then it is your responsibility to take care of you and the kids. Leave that person; get yourselves to safety. If that person is doing drugs and is out of their mind or could hurt you, call the police and get help. Get out of that bad situation. If that person has put you in a state of mind that is fearful or destructive then I am telling you to leave and get help! God would never tell you to put yourself in a situation that could get you hurt or would cause more harm. There are situations that we can not handle alone. This is where we are to love them from afar. Let them go and let God deal with them and their struggles until a change can be made in their hearts.

I believe that this is where I feel life with the Holy Spirit and the Lord is so vital. Because I feel like in my rationalization, in my heart, I feel like we could've loved our nephew a little longer. Maybe went to the courts and severed his parents completely from his life and he would've gotten better. Maybe we could've moved out of the area and made it harder for his parents to maintain the hold over him. BUT is that what God wanted us to do? As you can see, my mind is still trying to fix the problem. Even though it is legally no longer my responsibility to worry with. I still worry about this seventeen-year-old because we have invested in his future. We fed him. We clothed him. We spoke the Word of God over and to him. We bore the struggle for as long as we felt God had called us to. But it was our time to let him go and let God take the wheel in his life.

1 Corinthians 13:4-7: "Love is patient and kind; love does not envy or boast; it is not arrogant or rude. It does not insist on its own way; it is not irritable or resentful; it does not rejoice at wrongdoing, but rejoices with the truth. Love bears all things, believes all things, hopes all things, endures all things."

I rejoice in the truth that he will grow up eventually and he will know where the real love and the truth came from. My prayers and hopes for him and his life haven't ended just because the physical care and custody are no longer there. But it came to a point where fear was running our household and that could no longer be allowed. God does not want us to live in fear or submit to the spirit of fear in our lives.

1 John 4:18: "There is no fear in love, but perfect love casts out fear. For fear has to do with punishment, and whoever fears has not been perfected in love."

* * *

Ephesians 2:4-5: "God, being rich in mercy, because of the great love with which he loved us, even when we were dead in our trespasses, made us alive together with Christ - by grace you have been saved."

Because of God's mercy and love, He saved us from the life the world wanted for us. He saved us from a life of sin and death. He saved us from drugs, alcohol, or addiction. He saved us from ourselves. Ouch! Right? He saved us from a path of destruction and turned us onto a path of righteousness!

His love saved us from so much more destruction than we could've ever imagined. He saved us from the lies that were spoken over us. He saved us from the lies others have hurt us with. He saved us from ungodly, unhealthy love. He saved us from depression. He saved us from a life of feeling unworthy. He saved us from a life of generational curses. He saved us from fighting and warring with others. He saved us from hatred and anger. He saved us from a life that was never meant to be ours. He saved our marriages. He saved our friendships.

Ecclesiastes 4:9-12: "Two are better than one, because they have a good return for their labor: If either of them falls down, one can help the other up. But pity anyone who falls and has no one to help them up. Also, if two lie down together, they will keep warm. But how can one keep warm alone? Though one may be overpowered, two can defend themselves. A cord of three strands is not quickly broken."

Again I will say, He saved our friendships. If I could put a sound to describe what I feel in my soul to describe what I feel our church family should sound like, it would be the sound of marching. The sound of thousands of boots marching in perfect unison. March, March, March! Perfectly timed. Perfectly dressed. Perfectly carrying their weapons ready to go to war. March, March, March!

The closest I have physically ever been able to come to feeling this was in my high school years and I played in the marching band. My soul would sing every time we would march down from the high school to the field for a football game. I would hear the footsteps in unison marching down the hill on the road. I have had many family members who have served in the military. So I have always been drawn to some aspects of military life. The sharpness of the uniform. The discipline and reasoning to following orders. The repetition of the day-to-day duties and needs. But nothing gets my spirit jumping up and down like a platoon of marching soldiers. Or a group of people working together on a plan to overcome their struggles together.

If you can imagine with me, a platoon of men and women marching in unison. Heads facing upright and forward. Their arms and legs lift in the same accord. Their boots strike the ground creating a bass drum harmony to their movements. This is where my imagination sees the church body. All Christians marching to the same orders. Marching towards the same goal. Marching in the same war. Marching to see God's face and to hear, "Good Job! Good and faithful servant." If only marching together was all we had to perfect in God's request for perfection...We are called to be so much more because not everyone is as strong as the others. Not every soldier got the same life training experiences. God tells us we are different. We are all different because of our past experiences and temptations.

Our temptations are the tools the enemy uses to capture, bond, and keep us from being who God called us to be. Our temptations are what satan will use against us when we're walking the way God wants us to share His Great Message. While we're marching, we see so many today, are falling to the wayside. Succumbing to the lies of hurt and gossip. Leaving the church to hop to another click of "friends." So many Christians are allowing the enemy into their relationships. Instead of working with one another to fix and heal the problems. Learning from our mistakes and closing the gap the enemy tried to use against us. Allowing pride, fear, jealousy, envy, and anxiety to run a muck in their life. Allowing these spirits to tear them down and tear the platoon apart. When the enemy comes at one of your brothers and sisters we are called to hold them tight. Guard them with our shields. Lift them up. Pray for them. Cover them. Give them water to drink. We are called to nurse them back to health so that they can rejoin the ranks. We are called to step in front of the arrow meant to hurt them. We are called to lay down our life and squash the attack of the enemy.

* * *

1 John 3:16-18: "This is how we know what love is: Jesus Christ laid down his life for us. And we ought to lay down our lives for our brothers and sisters. If anyone has material possessions and sees a brother or sister in need but has no pity on them, how can the love of God be in that person? Dear children, let us not love with words or speech but with actions and in truth."

When we are linked arm and arm and in step with the will of the Father we are inseparable. We cannot be separated from the love of the Father and with His love we can love others just like He loved us. Because of His love, we changed from an addict to a healer. From a bar hopping partier to a stay-at-home loving mother. From a mean racist biker to a radical road warrior for the Lord. He has changed our lives for the better and now we can walk in the peace that He has given to us. When we submit our lives to the Lord then we submit our everything to Him. Our feet, our hands, our hearts, our minds. We are to give Him our all. For didn't Jesus give us His all when He dies on the cross for our sins?

Colossians 3:14: "And above all these put on love, which binds everything together in perfect harmony."

Philippians 4:9: "Whatever you have learned or received or heard from me, or seen in me—put it into practice. And the God of peace will be with you."

Romans 12:9-21: "Love must be sincere. Hate what is evil; cling to what is good. Be devoted to one another in love. Honor one another above yourselves. Never be lacking in zeal, but keep your spiritual fervor, serving the Lord. Be joyful in hope, patient in affliction, and faithful in prayer. Share with the Lord's people who are in need. Practice hospitality.

Bless those who persecute you; bless and do not curse. Rejoice with those who rejoice; mourn with those who mourn. Live in harmony with one another. Do not be proud, but be willing to associate with people of low positions. Do not be conceited.

Do not repay anyone evil for evil. Be careful to do what

is right in the eyes of everyone. If it is possible, as far as it depends on you, live at peace with everyone. Do not take revenge, my dear friends, but leave room for God's wrath, for it is written: "It is mine to avenge; I will repay," says the Lord. On the contrary:
"If your enemy is hungry, feed him;
if he is thirsty, give him something to drink.
In doing this, you will heap burning coals on his head."
Do not be overcome by evil, but overcome evil with good."

Although God is all-powerful, all-knowing, and very capable of defeating all the evil in this world, He has also given His Power to us to do in His Name. We can overcome evil by simply doing the opposite of what the world wants us to do. The World says we have every right to be ugly, nasty, upset, and angry. But God says for us to feed, them, give them water, shelter them, and love them. Despite all they have done to hurt you we are called to be their light in the storm. We are called to do good unto them and show them the way out of their darkness and lead them to Christ. That through our love and kindness they will see God. Until they accept Christ into their hearts they will never understand the will of God for them here on Earth.

Ephesians 5:6-20:
"Let no one deceive you with empty words, for because of such things God's wrath comes on those who are disobedient. Therefore do not be partners with them.
For you were once darkness, but now you are light in the Lord. Live as children of light (for the fruit of the light consists in all goodness, righteousness, and truth) and find out what pleases the Lord. Have nothing to do with the fruitless deeds of darkness, but rather expose them. It is shameful even to mention what the disobedient do in secret. But everything exposed by the light becomes visible—and everything that is illuminated becomes a light. This is why it is said:
"Wake up, sleeper, rise from the dead,
and Christ will shine on you."
Be very careful, then, how you live—not as unwise but as wise, making the most of every opportunity, because the days are

evil. **Therefore do not be foolish, but understand what the Lord's will is. Do not get drunk on wine, which leads to debauchery. Instead, be filled with the Spirit, speaking to one another with psalms, hymns, and songs from the Spirit. Sing and make music from your heart to the Lord, always giving thanks to God the Father for everything, in the name of our Lord Jesus Christ."**

2 Peter 3:9: "The Lord is not slow in keeping His promise, as some understand slowness. Instead, He is patient with you, not wanting anyone to perish, but everyone to come to repentance."

He wants everyone to come to repentance and to change from their evil ways. Even the ones who are hurting us. He loves and wants them to come to Him. He doesn't want them to die and perish in hell. So why would you think it would be okay for us to want that for them? If God loved us ALL that He gave us His only son to die on the cross for our sins then wouldn't He also want us to show love to one another just the same? I don't know about you but I can't imagine heaven with all of us, so-called Christians in the same place, trying to worship the Lord our God together! Mercy's sake we can't even agree on what theology is right. Let alone us trying to sing the same praise and worship song.

I can see the balcony to heaven right now. Jesus sitting at the right hand of the Father and the balcony encircled around the throne. Full of all the saints, prophets, disciples, and those loved ones who have gone before us. Looking down on our lives and shaking their head in shame...Could we share the goodness in us that was given by others to more people? Could we have helped that older woman to her car with all those groceries? Could we read a book to the kids at the elementary school? Could we play basketball with the boys at the youth center who don't have someone to play with? Could we give the girl in our Chemistry class mercy and grace for the wrongs she had committed? You see there are all kinds of deficits everywhere we look. We just have to produce the right kind of love inside our hearts to make a difference to others who need it.

You have to be honest about the love that you are showing. It is easy to love those friends and family members who are just like us. God says that even the tax collectors do that. God says that your love should be a grand gesture to bring them to His heart. Your love for others should be intentional. You can't accidentally love someone to a better life. For example, our love and peace that sinners will see and want to know more about Christ and how we can react this way despite all that life has done to us. Because to be honest with you, most people who are in the gutter have been told a lie one way or another as to why they are there and why they can't get out. They don't have enough money. They aren't white. They aren't black. They can't sing. They don't have the right look, hair, body, or physique. They are told lies to keep them in bondage and sin. They don't need any more condemnation. The enemy, satan, is already whispering enough of that into their ear.

What they need to hear is there is hope. They need to hear that they can do it. They need to hear that there is a way, a truth, and a life without the pain they have dealt with their whole lives. They need to hear that they are loved. They need to hear that they are worth the blood Christ gave for them. If we are God's chosen then it is our job to reach out and make sure they know these things. Most times it takes a little while before they will hear you. Sometimes it takes a meal or a sleeping bag. Sometimes it takes a note, a card, or a basketball game. Whatever it takes for us to let them know that they are going to be okay and that God loves them. Then it needs to be said and done. They need to hear the truth. They need to feel someone loves them honestly. They have felt satan's lies to the core; deep in their bones. So what they need now is to feel God's love wash over them. They need to have those lies and fears broken off of them. They need to know that you're not like the other people who have hurt them. That you're not trying to manipulate them. So again, Love them Honestly.

In this chapter I learned that I needed to love others honestly and in God's Truth. In reading this chapter I learned to love others despite what they had done to me. Did God reveal to you any new truths in His Scriptures here?

_____

_____

_____

_____

_____

_____

_____

_____

_____

How has God shown you that you can love them?

_____

_____

_____

_____

_____

_____

_____

_____

_____

Now let's pray this prayer together:

Dear Lord,
Thank you Lord for showing me that I am loved. Help me to see others with your eyes, to hug others with your peace, and to love others with your heart. Give me the strength to speak to the lies of the enemy over other people. Help me to know your words to speak

to them in their time of healing. Guide me to show others your truth. Walk with me as I move forward in your will for my life. Bring people into my path that will show me how I can share the gospel to. In Jesus' mighty name. Amen

"Little children, let us not love in word or talk but in deed and in truth." ~1 John 3:18

4

Chapter 4: Forgiveness

Can we stop here and can I be real for a moment? Writing this book has been hard for me. I have a lifetime of lessons learned and things that I have had to go through to give this testimony. Let me tell you the old saying is not true. Time does not heal all wounds. There are some strikes to the heart that have cut so deep that I still cringe at the thought of having to tell those enemies that I might forgive them... I said might. That's if I could ever bring myself to even talk to them. I'm still not sure I could ever do that. Needless to say, there are still some parts of my broken heart that are in the mixing dough phase. Parts to the broken pieces I knew had to be dealt with. Parts that I have cringed when God told me this was the next chapter of the book. As you can see, God is still working on me and my broken parts. I don't know much about what His end goal is for my life.

So let me write about what I do know regarding the matter.

Philippians 2:12-13:
"Therefore, my beloved, as you have always obeyed, so now, not only as in my presence but much more in my absence, work out your own salvation with fear and trembling, for it is God who works in you, both to will and to work for His good pleasure." (Let me clarify here there is only one God and it is HE in who we should fear. Fear His judgment.)

* * *

Although God's words are true and they will never return void in any situation. I sit here feeling pulled by the spirit to go deeper than the easy "go to His Biblical" answers. You know the scriptures that say we have to forgive because God forgave us? Or Love your enemies and do good to those who hate you. I still feel the Holy Spirit calling us to dig deeper into the Word. I could take you back to Adam and Eve, Cain and Able, or even Jacob and Esau. I could share with you their stories of disobeying, arguing, fighting and even killing each other over what was good and evil. But I want to take you to two different people in the Word who don't get talked about too often. Their stories are short but their message is abundantly clear.

The first person I want you to look and read about is a guy by the name of Hosea. If you want to read Hosea you must understand that to read it and truly understand it then you will have to go back to other books of the Bible to understand what Hosea is being asked to do and the problems he was facing. You have to understand the culture and lifestyle of the time when God is talking to Hosea. Like many other prophets and great Godly men or women in the Bible, the tasks God was asking them to do were always challenging. But in Hosea's case could be considered arguably horrifying. Theologists have speculated in regards to the actual timeline being perceived as wrong. That when he first married his wife she was not a prostitute. But please don't follow these tangents of distraction into your thoughts. Don't allow the enemy to steal God's revelation away from you. Read God's Word as it is written. As He has intended.

2 Timothy 3:16-18: "All Scripture *is* given by inspiration of God, and *is* profitable for doctrine, for reproof, for correction, for instruction in righteousness, that the man of God may be complete, thoroughly equipped for every good work."

Hosea was a prophet who was told by God to live his life according to the lessons God was teaching him about God's love for Israel and His people. Through Hosea's eyes, he was seeing and feeling exactly how God was feeling about God's people being unfaithful to

Him. God's people had lost their way. They were clinging to their unfaithful fathers' rule and Israel needed to be told to stop their perversions before it was too late. God was using Hosea to speak His warnings. Hosea had to live firsthand through God's hurt. God compared Israel's unfaithfulness to Hosea's wife. He even had to name their children names that professed the pain. Hosea pleads with Israel to come back to the Lord. To stop perverting themselves with false idols and rituals. God tells Hosea that He is going to bring down wrath upon Israel and they still choose to violate themselves with pagan idols.

I could only imagine the desperation felt deep in Hosea's soul for the people of Israel. Being a faithful servant and man of God. I imagine Hosea's time was no different than ours. Men of God have a stature about them. They carry God's mantle upon their lives. So I can only imagine that Hosea's heart broke into a thousand pieces when he was asked to marry Diblaim's daughter. Scripture tells us that she was a promiscuous woman. I don't know what promiscuous meant in Hosea's time, but I do know what it looks like in mine. Trashy, willing to do anything sexually for payment. She doesn't care if men touch her. She doesn't care that they want what they want. She doesn't care about God's standards of who a woman should be. She doesn't care about anything any longer. Her clothing was revealing her body. Her hair wasn't washed and clean. She didn't smell the greatest. She couldn't get better to be better. She was stuck being a whore.

So I can only imagine Hosea's heart and soul when he was asked to marry a woman such as her. God not only told him to marry her but to have children with her so that he could convey the warning Israel needed to repent. Could you only envision the ridicule the respectable men in the community gave Hosea? The hurt was caused by others in the community where he lived. The slander that was spoken about him behind his back. The ugliness their children felt because of who their mother was or more who she wasn't. She didn't care for them the way a nurturing woman would. A promiscuous woman could only think about what she wanted in her life. Who knows exactly what her eyes and body were after? Sex? Money? Status? Drugs? Alcohol?

So we can only conclude that Hosea and their children were without a woman who could love them the way they needed to be loved. Shoot, I don't know about you but when I don't get the love I need from my husband or family, I get a little upset. I get a little testy in my answers. I get a little frustrated, hurt, and bitter. Over time if it is not correctly dealt with it can come to a resentful hatred. A hardness where forgiveness and reconciliation almost are impossible. But as we read in Hosea God still pursues His Children. He still loves them. He still disciplines and corrects them. He is still chasing them back to Him. He still loves them regardless of the hurt, the adultery, the unfaithfulness, the sin. He forgave His Children for all they had done.

~*~

I want us to read about another saint in God's Word. His story was not even a long portion of the Bible. But it's a powerful one. The story of Stephen in **Acts 5-7**. After Christ had died and risen from the dead, the Holy Spirit was sent down to us. It wasn't easy becoming a Christian. Not only did it go against what the church said about being a believer but they had to speak out about their faith in believing in Christ. Not only were people fighting Rome for their ability to be a believer but now they were fighting the church on whether what they believed was even true. In a time when new believers were seeing and hearing the good news from the apostles themselves. The disciples knew that they alone could no longer carry this burden on their own. They discussed it and decided they were going to choose disciples of their own to take the ministry out further. In that harvest, Stephen was chosen. He excelled and was winning many hearts for the Lord. Enough that it caught the Jewish church's attention.

The Jews could not argue with Stephen. The Spirit of the Lord was on him and Stephen's wisdom was undeniable. So the church had some people lie and say Stephen was speaking blasphemy regarding Moses and against God. They bolstered the people and they called for his head. Stephen gives his last sermon on this day. His accounts and words were true and God tells us that Stephen died seeing God's face and seeing Jesus at the right hand of the father. Stephen was stoned to death right in the middle of the street by the people of God. Not killed by an addict in a back alley. Not killed for his money, car, or jewels. He was not killed because he was a bad guy already sent to jail for his sins. Oh No. He was killed by the church people.

He wasn't killed by street thugs, hardcore criminals, or even a distressed lover. He was killed by the very men claiming to follow after God's own heart. The men who supposedly lived their lives holy, pure, and righteous before all men. In that very moment, God's priests allowed satan's temptations of envy, jealousy, and pride to get to them. They allowed evil the right to work in their lives to justify murder.

Who are your temptations leading you to be? Is your temptation to pornography leading you to cheat on your wife? Is lying to your boss leading you to feel comfortable with leaving earlier than you're clocking out? How are your sins stealing your righteousness?

Luke 11:4: "Forgive us our sins, for we also forgive everyone who sins against us. And lead us not into temptation."

1 Timothy 6:9: "Those who want to get rich fall into temptation and a trap and into many foolish and harmful desires that plunge people into ruin and destruction."

We cry out to God asking how can we forgive them, Lord. How can we give them a pass on everything they have done to hurt us? They don't even care enough to ask for forgiveness for their hurtful words. They don't deserve it. That might be true according to your standards of life. But isn't that the point? That according to the value you have put on their story, forgiveness isn't in their cards. That they are so evil and the things that they have done have stolen your peace, your joy, your livelihood, your ability to go on living...But according to God, we don't need the motivation to forgive them. Aside from the fact that we once were all living in darkness; blind to the light and now we see it for what it truly is. Our sins are nothing more than a trap to keep us away from a healthy relationship with God.

Isaiah 59:1-2: "Behold, the Lord's hand is not shortened, that it cannot save, or His ear dull, that it cannot hear; but your iniquities have made a separation between you and your God, and

your sins have hidden his face from you so that He does not hear."

Matthew 6:14-15: "For if you forgive others their trespasses, your heavenly Father will also forgive you, but if you do not forgive others their trespasses, neither will your Father forgive your trespasses."

Galatians 6:1: "Brothers, if anyone is caught in any transgression, you who are spiritual should restore him in a spirit of gentleness. Keep watch on yourself, lest you too be tempted."

So although I can't find anything that says not forgiving someone is a sin, according to scripture it still separates us from the Father and our forgiveness. In the last chapter, we learned to love honestly with ourselves and with others. I feel the extension of God's love and mercy has followed us into this part of our lives. Forgiving others. But does it stop there? What else could the Father teach us about forgiveness?

~*~

If I have learned anything from the Father I have learned to never assume. You should never assume that God has nothing else to teach you. Because trust me, He will prove you wrong...

Our Bishop came to our church one week for services. I love it when he comes to worship with us because he always has a fresh outlook on our relationship with the Lord. I can't recall what he was ministering on but he told us a story of one of his accounts with the Lord. He was sitting one day with the Lord and working on a sermon on sin and in the middle of his notes God spoke and said you might want to deal with your issue with anger. Astonished he replied to God with denial and frustration. "God, I don't have a problem with anger." He went on about his day running errands. Out and about pulling into Wal-Mart's parking lot, he realized there was a nice parking spot free in front of the store. He pulled up to the spot and turned on his signal light to let others know he was pulling into this spot once the other driver was pulling out. Out of nowhere, a guy raced into the parking spot and took it before Bishop could pull in.

Angry and screaming Bishop got out of his car and went over to the other driver's window to give him a piece of his mind. The driver completely unaware of the situation turned to get out of his car and realized bishop was standing there upset and began to roll down his window. "I'm sorry, Pastor. Is there something wrong?" Bishop completely unaware he had his bishop collar on was mortified and went on about his way. So if God tells you that you have an issue and to deal with it, make sure you heed his warning.

So again what more could God teach us about forgiveness? I was taken to the scripture. If you are not seeing the pattern in my life is that God's word is where we can find all our answers.

John 15:5: "I am the vine; you are the branches. Whoever abides in me and I in him, he it is that bears much fruit, for apart from me you can do nothing."

I was a young adult in Bible school at church and we were learning about the Fruits of the Spirit. It is the verse that always comes to mind when I am looking inward and judging who I am in the Lord. Am I producing good fruits? It is the balance of the scales that keeps my mind and heart on God's path. I judge it by my fruits. Are the words of correction to my daughter producing love or anger? Is the way I am talking to my coworkers encouraging and uplifting or are they pulling away from me? Is the way I am explaining something to my husband comforting or is he getting mad? It's always about the fruit. If it is not producing Fruits of the Spirit then does it need to be spoken?

So I began searching deep inside. Inspecting my heart and soul. Although there were promising fruits on the surface, the underlying ground had crusted over. The ground was callused and hard. Deep down I knew that the ground couldn't breathe anymore. This, to me, was a funny way to describe it because in my real life, my health was failing and breathing was such a chore for me. No explanation. Doctors couldn't figure it out. Everyone kept attributing my breathing issues to my heart, but my spirit just kept screaming something different. All that was doing was making me frustrated.

Back to how I felt inside...There was a big difference one year can make. In two years I was a different person. Two years prior I was relying on God to provide everything. All my hard work had done was replace my knowledge of God's provision and somehow I began relying on myself. To the present where I was, I would describe my life as destitute, unsure, and unable how to move forward. Unsure how I let God down that He would take everything away. Two years ago the prayers I had for my business were being answered. Things finally felt like they were moving forward. I felt like the accumulation of everything God had taught me was finally going to be released. That God was going to use me and I was going to be able to walk in my purpose. I had sat for so long. Waiting on God to release me to be who He called me to be. So when I finally opened my storefront I was able to get to work and get busy.

However, somewhere along the way and the harshness of being a new business owner with unreliable employees I slowly but surely began to concentrate on the work more than who God wanted me to be. It's hard enough just trying to be me daily, but try being yourself, the cashier, the marketing person, the billing person, the estimate person, the caterer, the baker, the janitor, the cleaner, the mom, the feeder, the only person doing everything. For two years I searched for others who could help me make this business run like a well-oiled machine. But once I found a good cashier and moved on to find a good baker, it always seemed I could never have the two stations filled with good people. So I spent the majority of the last two years doing it all myself. I was exhausted, frustrated, and upset most of my time away from work. Without spending the time needed to remain close to God I slowly became useless to anyone. Especially to God.

I look back on this time with more regrets than I really would like to admit. But my biggest mistake was getting too busy for my alone time with God. Many things can be blamed. It was the heavy workload's fault. The staff weren't reliable enough. If I am being truly honest, no one can be blamed except for myself. I went from sitting still and completely bored with life to not having enough time to spend with God. Not enough energy to make it to any extra church services. Not enough time to bake extra goodies for my loving church family. Just not enough hands to get it all done. There wasn't enough of me to go around. When all I had to do was keep my head focused on the way maker. Focused on more of God.

All I could ever get done was never enough and I always felt like there just wasn't enough time in my day to get it completed.

I'm sure that if my heart would've been more focused on God, the Holy Spirit would have warned me that I was heading down a destructive pathway. But in my recklessness, I let go of God and concentrated on nothing but my work. House, kid, work, feed the kid, drive home, feed the kid, and repeat.

God tells us in **Colossians 3:2: "Set your minds on things that are above, not on things that are on earth."**

That if we set our minds on Him we will not fall into the trap of temptation or destruction.

Romans 8:5: "For those who live according to the flesh set their minds on the things of the flesh, but those who live according to the Spirit set their minds on the things of the Spirit. For to set the mind on the flesh is death, but to set the mind on the Spirit is life and peace. For the mind that is set on the flesh is hostile to God, for it does not submit to God's law; indeed, it cannot. Those who are in the flesh cannot please God."

According to this scripture, how can we put anything or anyone before the Lord? Why would we want to? Yet, we do it every day. We put all our energies into making money, buying things for the kids, and working hard so we can go to the beach, the lake, or hunting. We play so hard on Saturday that we can't find the energy to get up and go to church on Sunday. We listen to secular music on our car radios because our Christian station can no longer be reached. We make excuses to allow the enemy to come into our lives; when clearly God told us to separate ourselves from it. That according to scripture we are heading towards death if we live by the flesh. If we give in to the temptations and live by the flesh then we fall short of the glory of God and push Him further away.

How could I have let anything come before God? How could I think that anything was more important than my time with Him? I didn't walk away from Him. I just slowly stopped talking with Him. Stopped listening to Him guide me. Slowly allowed bitterness, frustration, and anger to be the emotions I would rush to in a stressful situation. Instead of calling on the Lord and living in peace and wisdom. You see I didn't knowingly push God away. I didn't reject or deny Him. I slowly allowed other things to become more important than my relationship and time with Him. I allowed my responsibilities to overshadow my love for my Lord. Without even knowing I was doing so, but looking back the fruits that I was producing didn't feel righteous. I had fallen into the enemy's trap. I could barely believe my heart and eyes. I was unforgivable. How could I let this happen after all I had already come through?

~*~

Remember at the beginning of the chapter when I wondered what more about forgiveness could God need to teach me, and I said don't tell God you don't have an issue with something... Leave it to God to show you the truth. It wasn't my old enemies, or the people who had hurt me, or the ones who had done me wrong that I couldn't forgive. It was me. I had to learn to forgive myself for allowing the enemy into my life. I didn't mean to but I had chosen to go after something other than God. To say it was anything else would be a lie.

If I look to the scriptures the way I had done every other question in my life, then I would find the truth. Why was I striving to work so hard? Was it for money? Provision? God has the answer.

Philippians 4:19: "And my God will supply every need of yours according to His riches in glory in Christ Jesus."

Psalms 37:4: "Delight yourself in the Lord, and he will give you the desires of your heart."

Luke 12:28-31: "But if God so clothes the grass, which is alive in the field today, and tomorrow is thrown into the oven, how much more will he clothe you, O you of little faith! And do not seek what you are to eat and what you are to drink, nor be worried. For all the nations of the world seek after these things, and your Father knows that you need them. Instead, seek his kingdom, and these things will be added to you."

Matthew 6:31-33: "Therefore do not be anxious, saying, 'What shall we eat?' or 'What shall we drink?' or 'What shall we

wear?' For the Gentiles seek after all these things, and your heavenly Father knows that you need them all. But seek first the kingdom of God and His righteousness, and all these things will be added to you."

Money doesn't feel like enough of an answer. What else was behind the motivation? Was it pride? Fear of failure? Fear of being without a way to provide for myself? Anxiety that I wasn't providing for my house as much as my husband was? Or maybe I wanted to be someone more important than I was. I wanted to be someone more worthy than I felt like I was. Someone hurtful once spoke over me that I would never be anything more than who I was (as they looked me up and down in disgust) without him and his family. That I would never be able to take care of my daughter and myself. That his mother and father would have to rent me one of their trailers just to provide me with a roof over our heads.

I know, ouch. Right? Don't worry. I know how it feels to have hurtful words said to you. I know how sad, angry, and vengeful words can make you feel. I can also tell you hurtful words can stick with you for a very long time. Regardless, of how well you think you can shrug them off or justify the reasoning was because the evil person who spoke them was a tyrant or monster. Words are evil spirits all of their own. God speaks of their power with great warning.

Proverbs 15:4: "A gentle tongue is a tree of life, but perverseness in it breaks the spirit."

Matthew 15:18: "But what comes out of the mouth proceeds from the heart, and this defiles a person."

James 3:5: "So also the tongue is a small member, yet it boasts of great things. How great a forest is set ablaze by such a small fire!"

Proverbs 18:21: "Death and life are in the power of the tongue, and those who love it will eat its fruits."

That last scripture always throws a hitch in my giddyup. I have, because of the person who spoke such mean things over me, had such a bad self-image of myself. I'm not sexy anymore. I am not pretty anymore. I am fat, ugly and no one wants me anymore. I spoke more hurtful things over myself than my worst enemy ever could. If scripture tells us the truth is life then I have been killing myself for years! Isn't that what the enemy wants from us? To kill, steal and destroy us? The need I had to forgive myself for the ugly things I had spoken over myself only watered the evil seed that was planted in my heart by others. It was slowly leading to the decrease of God in my life. My soul was crushed.

Psalm 34:18: "The Lord is near to the brokenhearted and saves the crushed in spirit."
Psalms 147:3: "He heals the brokenhearted and binds up their wounds."

1 Peter 2:24: "He himself bore our sins in His body on the tree, that we might die to sin and live to righteousness. By His wounds, you have been healed."

There are so many of us who have been hurt by someone who should have loved us and should have been truthful with us. That person was my Dad or that person was my husband. They should have been our protectors. They should have loved us more than anyone else on Earth. They should have never done those hurtful things to us. But how many of us are taking the identity of the person who hurt us and using it against others? My Dad hurt me and therefore God can't be my Father because all fathers are now bad. Or are you thinking my husband cheated on me and left us with nothing so now all men aren't worth anything? Or my last church pastor lied to us and took our money, so now all churches are bad and I don't need church people to know God. I'm fine without them in my life anymore. Allowing unforgiveness to rule our thoughts will affect everything that God is saying about our futures.

I had to learn to forgive my ex-husband and I had to learn to forgive myself for allowing the evil one to use me and my work for his desires in my life. I had to ask the Father to forgive me for allowing him to do this to us. I had to go straight to Him and ask for forgiveness. I had to repent.

Repentance.

In this chapter, I learned that it was vital to forgive others for the hurts they had caused me but more importantly, I had to learn how to forgive myself for the negative things I had continued to speak over myself. I learned my negative words were not God's truths over my life. Did God reveal any important truths about forgiveness to you in this chapter?

_____
_____
_____
_____
_____
_____
_____
_____
_____
_____
_____

Please pray this prayer with me today:

Dear Lord,

Today I learned that I had to forgive myself for the negative words I was speaking over my life that were not your truths for me. Help me Lord to forgive myself for these hurtful things. Give me the scriptures to stand upon that will reveal your truths of how important I am to you. Send people into my life that will always speak your positivity over me. Guide me as I break off these negative thoughts and put on your armor of truth and righteousness. In Jesus' mighty name. Amen

"But what comes out of the mouth proceeds from the heart, and this defiles a person." ~Matthew 15:18

5

Chapter 5: Real Repentance

2 Chronicles 7:14: "If my people who are called by my name humble themselves, and pray and seek my face and turn from their wicked ways, then I will hear from heaven and will forgive their sin and heal their land."

One of the first things we learn when we are introduced to the Lord is we have all done things that were against God's Laws and that we come short of His approval. That the only way we can ever achieve holiness and be with Him; to fellowship with Him is to repent by asking Him to forgive us of those sins against Him. He tells us in His Word that He will forgive us and our names will be written into the Book of Life. That after that repentance we can talk to Him, be guided by Him, and fellowship with Him. Then He will show us a better life through Him. So here we are converted sinners; learning all we can about God and how we are supposed to sound, look and talk just like His Son, Jesus Christ.

We change our habits, our routines, and our lives to adjust to a new life in Christ. We put our sinful ways in our past and move constantly towards a future with Christ leading the way. But wait a second, then why aren't we overflowing in sunshine and rainbows? There are many references to sins and ugly things people can do to other people. The five o'clock news from our everyday life couldn't be a better example of all these horrible acts. But yet, it still feels like there is more to it than just that. Have you ever walked away from an incident or experienced wondering where in the heck that came from? Or wondered how that just happened? I have. I have been through some crazy experiences that should make someone wonder about the tormenting demons that are influencing our lives. However, as I am writing this chapter and want to tell you more about the craziness I have been through, I keep coming across this one scripture with the Holy Spirit's warning in my heart.

Leviticus 19:31: **"Do not turn to mediums or necromancers; do not seek them out, and so make yourselves unclean by them: I am the Lord your God."**

The Holy Spirit keeps telling me to stay away from finding out more about the evil presence in the world. I had this whole chapter somewhat planned out and I was going to call out some demons active in the church and our lives today. I was going to give you characteristics about these evil presences and tell you all the signs so that you know what demon you were dealing with and what you should do about them…But God keeps saying, "NO!" "Don't glorify the enemy by promoting his evildoers." Which is so true. By talking about evil spirits in the details of my experiences I am doing nothing more than drawing attention to the hurtful and evil ways already in the world. So we don't want to do that. So we are going to be obedient and stay away from finding out more about the spirit world…

God tells us in Leviticus that we are not to search those things out. By learning about them it invites an open door for the evil to come into operate in our lives. Now please don't be confused. When you asked Christ to come into your heart and to be your Lord and Savior then you vacated the enemy's right to ever come into your soul. A Christian cannot be possessed by any demons or deities. You were bought and paid for with the blood of Jesus Christ who died for your sins on the cross. By giving your heart to the Lord no evil spirit can come into your body. But I do want to forewarn you there are evil spirits out there and their mission is to come and to kill, steal and destroy. They can't posses you but they can whisper in your ear. They can talk to you. They can distort how you think or perceive things or situations. So when your situation is going out of control and you can't make sense of the chaos make sure you are heading in the right direction to deal with those problems. My answer is to always turn to the Lord. Ask Him to come into your home or workplace and clean out any spirits that are operating in evil and causing problems. It's only in Jesus' name that we can clean out those evil spirits and rid ourselves of their torment.

Ephesians 6:10-12: "Finally, be strong in the Lord and in the strength of his might. Put on the whole armor of God, that you may be able to stand against the schemes of the devil. For we do not wrestle against flesh and blood, but against the rulers, against the authorities, against the cosmic powers over this present darkness, against the spiritual forces of evil in the heavenly places."

In any situation, we have the opportunity to assess the perspective that we choose to concentrate on. We can set our minds on the good or wrong that is happening around us. For example, someone you work with has been sad and depressed. They are going through a bad divorce and everything in the world is just wrong. They choose to complain and focus on the bad things that are happening in the world. All they do all day is find things that are not right and demand that they be fixed. So we could go into work with an ugly, mean attitude and make their life a living hell even more or we could go in and concentrate on the good and try to be the Light of God to Him. Maybe we could ask him how he's doing. Try to help him get through this rough time with a shoulder for him to lean on. Remember, guys counsel guys. Females only counsel females. We don't want to put ourselves in a compromising situation that will come back to burn us later.

When I was going through my ugly divorce, I found myself concentrating on the bad things my ex-husband was doing. It was all I could think of. I couldn't make sense of why the courts were allowing these horrible things to happen. Our justice system was supposed to be this checked and balanced system to keep justice true, fair, and righteous. But that was not what was at work in my case. Everything was out of wack. Guardian Ad Litem was misrepresenting my child. Attorneys were acting like the devil himself during court proceedings. Screaming and accusing my pastors on the stand.

Friends were suddenly ugly and hurtful. Family disowning me and telling me there was something not right with me because I wouldn't key his car, scream, yell, and fight. Strangers messaging me on Facebook saying hurtful and disrespectful things. When all I was trying to do was do what God kept telling me to do. Be still. It wasn't until I came across scripture about different spirits at work in the world that my eyes and heart started to see a different perspective.

2 Corinthians 11:14-15: "And no wonder, for even satan disguises himself as an angel of light. So it is no surprise if his servants, also, disguise themselves as servants of righteousness. Their end will correspond to their deeds."

There was evil in the world pretending to be good and righteous. It was like there was a heavy fog over my eyes and now I could see the truth for what it really was. Now years later, I have crossed paths with many of these people and they have apologized and have said they didn't know why they did that or why they didn't see the situation for what it really was. So if there are evil servants in the world pretending to be for us, then how do we know who to trust? How do we know who has the good in our future in their actions? This is where I found myself in the truth. I found myself not only exposing the lies but my purpose here is to give you a way to defend yourselves against these fiery attacks.

Ephesians 6:10-20: "Take up the shield of faith, with which you can extinguish all the flaming arrows of the evil one."

These fiery arrows are sent into our lives to cause our home, our shelter, and our peaceful place to go up in a raging fire that can never be healed. If you read the book I suggested by Dr. Charles Stanley, you would remember that those fiery arrows are what he calls the attacks of satan on our life. Every evil temptation is an attack on your heart, your mind, your home, and your relationships. On your holiness.

Every temptation that comes against you is what satan is trying to use to ruin your life is a chance for you to either give in and go down like an oil rig in a train wreck or you can rise above the attack and come out of the furnace without a scratch. Like the three who were punished for praying to the one true God. Their names were Daniel, Hananiah, Mishael, and Azariah. Their new king didn't want them to have Hebrew names so he gave them new names. Daniel was given the name of Belteshazzar, and to Hananiah was called Shadrach, and to Mishael was called Meshach, and Azariah was called Abednego. Shadrach, Meshach, and Abednego were three Jews; God's chosen people whose kingdom was taken over by the Chaldeans. When the king was taking captives he had decided that he wanted all the clean and unblemished children to be brought into his palace to be trained to learn their language and their ways. Daniel or Belteshazzar decided that he was not going to defile himself by taking their sinful ways into his life. So according to Daniel 1 and 2, these four men proved themselves in the eyes of the priests and kings. They would not eat or drink the king's foods to keep themselves pure. They also prayed to God during specific times of day and the king's heralds, governors and rulers did not like the fact that they were given special treatment over them. So they manipulated the king to decree a new law that would make everyone in the kingdom have to bow down to a golden statue of him or face death in the fiery furnace. Convicted of God's Truths over them, they refused to bow down to any other idols or gods and were sentenced to death.

Daniel 3:16-17: "**Shadrach, Meshach, and Abednego, answered and said to the king, O Nebuchadnezzar, we are not careful to answer thee in this matter.**
If it is so, our God whom we serve can deliver us from the burning fiery furnace, and He will deliver us out of thine hand, O king."

Needless to say, they never bowed down to the statue and were put into the fiery furnace. The king was so upset that they wouldn't listen to him that he made the furnace seven times hotter than normal as their punishment. It's like satan thought that he finally had them pushed them into the corner and could force them to finally do evil. He knew they would worship the false idol. Who in the world would want to die such a horrible death? Of course, they had to sin against God. They had no other choice, right? No! They had a choice and their choice was to choose to serve the one and true only living God. At the end of their story when they were thrown into the fiery furnace. However, God saved them. Nebuchadnezzar, the king himself could see the three men inside the fire; unharmed and joined by a fourth person who looked like the Son of God. These men took on a full attack of satan plus his fiery death and came out of the furnace unharmed. No flame harmed them. They didn't even smell like the smoke! All that had been changed were the binds that held their hands burned away. They were free! They were free to worship their true, one and only Living God.

It didn't keep the enemy (the enemy being satan) from coming against them. It didn't stop satan from trying to take their freedom; or their lives. In my experience, it's God's righteousness that makes others so mad at you. It's easier to live in sin and evil if you wear a mask that keeps others from seeing the evil operating in your life. God's light that lives inside Christians will unmask evil in others all around you. We can see evil for what it truly is. We can see it operating in its true form. Our eyes are unveiled to see the truth. We are given this ability to see these things so that we can reach others, calling out the evil that is operating in these situations and helping them to see the truth. We are given wisdom and discernment so that we can see the fiery arrows and extinguish them before they can cause harm to ourselves or others. There is no greater plan in war than seeing what your opponent is up to and avoiding his destructive escapades.

That is why we are to fellowship with other Christians is so important; so that we can learn from others and receive counsel as needed. We can't always see what the enemy is up to when we are so entrenched with emotions. Having others linked to the Father to help us on this journey is just what the heavenly Father called for. Sinners don't see the world as we do. They justify their sins and actions on whether or not it is good or bad because they've never been caught. It isn't against the law to look at pornography on the computer, or movies, or magazines. It's not even against the law to cheat on your spouse. But the harm that it causes to your marriage and to your children is unfathomable. It isn't against the law to drink alcohol. But the harm that it causes the mind and body is deadly. It isn't against the law to be envious of a neighbor's new car or hot wife. But the harm it causes your inner peace is detrimental. It isn't against the law to smoke cigarettes. But the harm it causes your body and loved ones around you is destructive.

People who are not walking in a close relationship with the Lord can't see the fiery arrows coming at them. They can't see that the girl at the workplace that is flirting with them is on a path to losing their home, car, wife, and kids in a custody battle. They can't see the alcohol is going to cause them to get into a car wreck and will kill another family in the accident. They don't see the pack-a-day cigarettes they choose to smoke is going to lead them to lung cancer and they'll die at an early age.

You see, God's "rules" are here to keep you from falling into the destructive ways of sin laid before you by the enemy. God tells us not to partake of these evil things because they lead us to death. He wants your future to be good. He wants you to live. He wants your family to be happy. He wants you to be free from a life of bondage that sin creates in your life. He wants you to be set free from the jail cell that the sin will cause your life.

Romans 8:2: "For the law of the Spirit of life has set you free in Christ Jesus from the law of sin and death."

Jeremiah 29:11-13: "For I know the plans I have for you, declares the Lord, plans for welfare and not for evil, to give you a future and a hope. Then you will call upon me and come and pray to me, and I will hear you. You will seek me and find me when you seek me with all your heart."

Ephesians 5:8: "For at one time you were in darkness, but now you are light in the Lord. Walk as children of light."

John 12:35: "So Jesus said to them, "The light is among you for a little while longer. Walk while you have the light, lest darkness overtake you. The one who walks in the darkness does not know where he is going."

How do we know where we are going? How do we know where we are supposed to go? How do we know which way is our true path to righteousness? The easiest answer I can give is to start with the Ten Commandments. If there was any truer way to the righteousness of God, then I have not yet found it. Repenting for any of these sins is the only real path to becoming holy before the Lord.

Exodus 20:

"And God spoke all these words:

[2] "I am the Lord your God, who brought you out of Egypt, out of the land of slavery.

[3] "You shall have no other gods before me.

[4] "You shall not make for yourself an image in the form of anything in heaven above or on the earth beneath or in the waters below. [5] You shall not bow down to them or worship them; for I, the Lord your God, am a jealous God, punishing the children for the sin of the parents to the third and fourth generation of those who hate me, [6] but showing love to a thousand generations of those who love me and keep my commandments.

[7] "You shall not misuse the name of the Lord your God, for the Lord will not hold anyone guiltless who misuses his name.

[8] "Remember the Sabbath day by keeping it holy. [9] Six days you shall labor and do all your work, [10] but the seventh day is a sabbath to the Lord your God. On it you shall not do any work, neither you, nor your son or daughter, nor your male or female servant, nor your animals, nor any foreigner residing in your towns. [11] For in six days the Lord made the heavens and the earth, the sea, and all that is in them, but he rested on the seventh day. Therefore the Lord blessed the Sabbath day and made it holy.

[12] "Honor your father and your mother, so that you may live long in the land the Lord your God is giving you.

[13] "You shall not murder.

[14] "You shall not commit adultery.

[15] "You shall not steal.

[16] "You shall not give false testimony against your neighbor.

[17] "You shall not covet your neighbor's house. You shall not covet your neighbor's wife, or his male or female servant, his ox or donkey, or anything that belongs to your neighbor."

[18] When the people saw the thunder and lightning and heard the trumpet and saw the mountain in smoke, they trembled with fear. They stayed at a distance [19] and said to Moses, "Speak to us

yourself and we will listen. But do not have God speak to us or we will die."

[20] Moses said to the people, "Do not be afraid. God has come to test you, so that the fear of God will be with you to keep you from sinning."

[21] The people remained at a distance, while Moses approached the thick darkness where God was.

[22] Then the Lord said to Moses, "Tell the Israelites this: 'You have seen for yourselves that I have spoken to you from heaven: [23] Do not make any gods to be alongside me; do not make for yourselves gods of silver or gods of gold. "

For any sane, good, and productive member of society, most of these commandments are easy for us to follow. Most Christians can quote these verses by heart. We hold our heads high, knowing that we are good and faithful Christians. Worthy of HIS Praise. But Jesus Christ tells us that to even think about the evil act because we might as well have done the act itself. Any seed planted in our hearts can grow into a destructive harmful light-blocking vine in us. If we allow it.

Matthew 5:28: "But I say to you that everyone who looks at a woman with lustful intent has already committed adultery with her in his heart."

Matthew 12:34: "You brood of vipers! How can you speak good, when you are evil? For out of the abundance of the heart the mouth speaks."

James 1:26: "If anyone thinks he is religious and does not bridle his tongue but deceives his heart, this person's religion is worthless."

So how do we remain on our path of righteousness if even God says that if we think it then we have sinned? The answer is to train our minds to capture those thoughts and give them to the Lord and let Him dispose of them. For my path, I fight daily with those thoughts of unworthiness. I am not depressed but I have a very low self-esteem. I have to capture those negative thoughts and words every second of the day. Sometimes every half second. I have to remind myself that I am worthy, capable, and wanted. Again, reminding myself that I can't allow the enemy into my mind to cause harm. I have to remind myself to go to God's Word and speak God's truth over me. I have to encourage myself in the Lord. I have to go and sit in His presence and talk with Him. I have to put on my praise and worship. I have to spend time in my Word to bring myself closer to Him. He tells us in **James 4:8** that if we draw nearer to Him then He will draw nearer to us. Sometimes I have to ask my husband to speak God's truths over me. It always feels better and more spiritually uplifting to hear that someone else loves me. Not just God, but that another human being believes in me. That's where surrounding yourself with other Christians is good for the mind, body, and soul.

Hebrews 4:12: "For the Word of God is living and active, sharper than any two-edged sword, piercing to the division of soul and spirit, of joints and of marrow, and discerning the thoughts and intentions of the heart."

God's Word is the weapon we must always refer to destroy those bad thoughts. To come in and extinguish the fiery arrow before it can cause real harm. God tells us it will cut through the soul and spirit. God will take those captured thoughts and rip the shadow of them that we are connected to. He will send them back to where they came from. Where ever that might be.

Ephesians 5:11: "Take no part in the unfruitful works of darkness, but instead expose them."

Unfruitful.

To me, that was the biggest word in that scripture. As a Christian, I have taken great happiness knowing I hadn't committed an unpardonable sin. You know. Murder...Stealing... Actual Idol Building. But this word in this scripture struck me hard. Unfruitful... Were the words I was speaking over myself fruitful? If we are allowing God's Word to guide us on our path to righteousness then were the words of negativity and low self-esteem actually producing the Fruits of the Spirit that were being used to describe myself? Were these harmful words pointing others to God and were they a positive influence over their lives? If I applied the same applications to my thoughts and words over myself, did they bring joy, happiness, peace, and love? Were they drawing me closer to the Lord? Or were they pushing me away from Him? Did they agree with God's Words about how HE feels about me? My answer was a hard no. Those negative words only brought forth more negative thoughts and feelings. Then they have to stop. Repentance.

Psalm 15:1-5: "A Psalm of David. O Lord, who shall sojourn in your tent? Who shall dwell on your holy hill? He who walks blamelessly and does what is right and speaks truth in his heart; who does not slander with his tongue and does no evil to his neighbor, nor takes up a reproach against his friend; in whose eyes a vile person is despised, but who honors those who fear the Lord; who swears to his own hurt and does not change; who does not put out his money at interest and does not take a bribe against the innocent. He who does these things shall never be moved."

2 Corinthians 7:1: "Since we have these promises, beloved, let us cleanse ourselves from every defilement of body and spirit, bringing holiness to completion in the fear of God."

Galatians 5:19-21: "Now the works of the flesh are evident: sexual immorality, impurity, sensuality, idolatry, sorcery, enmity, strife, jealousy, fits of anger, rivalries, dissensions, divisions, envy, drunkenness, orgies, and things like these. I warn you, as I warned you before, that those who do such things will not inherit the kingdom of God."

It is here that I have found myself asking, God how many times will He forgive us for our sins? God's love has no limitation but even in scripture we read about the end of His grace and mercy. Look at Noah, or the unholy city of Sodom and Gomorrah, or the story of Jonah and Nineveh...All of these accounts were parts of history where unrepentant people were warned of their demise if they continued in their sinful ways. Some heeded their warning and lived. However, others ignored God's Prophets and they tossed the warning aside recklessly. Unafraid of God and what He says He will do. Unafraid of the consequences of their actions. Unafraid of the results of sin and death in their life. Unafraid of the hurt that the sin was causing their life. Unafraid of a loving God begging them to repent and turn from their ways.

Why are we afraid of our parents when we are disciplined? Is it because we are afraid of the butt-whooping that could come upon us? Or is there a greater fear that lies beneath the surface? It is because we are afraid of losing the relationship we have together. We are afraid of losing their trust and their respect. We are afraid of losing the love. We have lost the fear of losing God's love in our lives.

In this chapter, I learned that repentance was important because it is vital to the change that has to happen in our lives to bring us closer to God. Through forgiveness and repentance, we can heal. With God's love, we can move forward in His Wisdom. I learned that God's rules were there to help me and protect me from the death that sin can bring. Did God reveal any new truths about repentance for you in this chapter?

_____

_____

_____

_____

_____

_____

_____

_____

_____

_____

_____

Now pray this prayer with me:

Dear Lord,

I am so sorry for the sins that I have committed in my life revealed to me by your Word. Please forgive me for those sins against you. I repent for the part I played in believing the lies the enemy has spoken over me. I ask for your forgiveness right now. Help me to move forward in your truth in my life. Guide me as I heal and help me to resist the temptations to continue these sins throughout my life. In Jesus' mighty name. Amen

6

Chapter 6: Fear of God

Psalm 103:13: "As a father shows compassion to His children, so the Lord shows compassion to those who fear Him."

As a parent, it is our "job" to correct, discipline, and change our children's attitudes or behaviors for the greater good. It's at our discretion how we teach these lessons. We move forward hoping they learn them with ease and without drastic measures. Not all parents get the luxury of a well-behaved child. However, not all lessons can be easily taught. So many variables are needed to effectively get our points across to our kids.

With my first daughter, from the day she was born, all I had to do was give her an unapproving tone in my voice not do something and she would turn from what she was doing and would listen to my warning. She was easy to teach and would catch on to lessons with great ease and a joyful spirit. My second daughter is the exact opposite. Every lesson with her usually requires a declaration of war, a surrender of goods or possessions, then a white flag to signify the conceding of her will before we could even get her to think about listening to what we were asking her to do. Every child is different and as I said, many different variables are taken into consideration for a desired effect. With our children we have to consider whether or not they're hungry, whether have they had their diaper changed, whether or not they're thirsty, whether or not they are sleepy, and whether or not they have had any other influences like TV shows, games, or friends influencing their thought processes and that's not even considering their biological makeup.

As their mother, the methods may differ but the reason is still the same. I love and cherish both of them the same. Regardless of how different they are to me, my love still overcomes any other emotion I may feel. I may have to spend more time and effort with my second daughter because of her strong-willed passion to not listen but I don't love or care for them any differently. My love still motivates my decisions on how to discipline them and I feel very strongly that God feels the very same way about each of us. We were all raised differently. Different variables created our stories and many different ingredients were added to our mixtures to create our voices. But He adopted us into His Kingdom Family for His Glory all equally.

Ephesians 1:5: "For He chose us in Him before the creation of the world to be holy and blameless in His sight. In love, He predestined us for adoption to sonship through Jesus Christ, in accordance with His pleasure and will— to the praise of His glorious grace, which He has freely given us in the One He loves."

Each child learns differently. We are disciplined and corrected in different ways. Every person written about in the Bible had a different method of motivation behind every instruction but the reason for the lesson was the same. God loved them and wanted them to be with Him again. He wanted them to be holy.

Look at the story of Jonah and Nineveh.

1 The word of the Lord came to Jonah son of Amittai: "Go to the great city of Nineveh and preach against it, because its wickedness has come up before me."

But Jonah ran away from the Lord and headed for Tarshish. He went down to Joppa, where he found a ship bound for that port. After paying the fare, he went aboard and sailed for Tarshish to flee from the Lord.

Then the Lord sent a great wind on the sea, and such a violent storm arose that the ship threatened to break up. All the sailors were afraid and each cried out to his own god. And they threw the cargo

into the sea to lighten the ship.

But Jonah had gone below deck, where he lay down and fell into a deep sleep. The captain went to him and said, "How can you sleep? Get up and call on your god! Maybe he will take notice of us so that we will not perish."

Then the sailors said to each other, "Come, let us cast lots to find out who is responsible for this calamity." They cast lots and the lot fell on Jonah. [8] So they asked him, "Tell us, who is responsible for making all this trouble for us? What kind of work do you do? Where do you come from? What is your country? From what people are you?"

He answered, "I am Hebrew and I worship the Lord, the God of heaven, who made the sea and the dry land."

This terrified them and they asked, "What have you done?" (They knew he was running away from the Lord, because he had already told them so.)

The sea was getting rougher and rougher. So they asked him, "What should we do to you to make the sea calm down for us?"

"Pick me up and throw me into the sea," he replied, "and it will become calm. I know that it is my fault that this great storm has come upon you."

Instead, the men did their best to row back to land. But they could not, for the sea grew even wilder than before. Then they cried out to the Lord, "Please, Lord, do not let us die for taking this man's life. Do not hold us accountable for killing an innocent man, for you, Lord, have done as you pleased." Then they took Jonah and threw him overboard, and the raging sea grew calm. At this, the men greatly feared the Lord, and they offered a sacrifice to the Lord and made vows to him.

Jonah's Prayer

Now the Lord provided a huge fish to swallow Jonah, and Jonah was in the belly of the fish for three days and three nights.

From inside the fish, Jonah prayed to the Lord his God. He said:

"In my distress, I called to the Lord,

and he answered me.

From deep in the realm of the dead I called for help,

and you listened to my cry.

You hurled me into the depths,

into the very heart of the seas,
  and the currents swirled about me;
all your waves and breakers
  swept over me.
I said, 'I have been banished
  from your sight,
yet I will look again
  toward your holy temple.'
The engulfing waters threatened me,[b]
  the deep surrounded me;
  seaweed was wrapped around my head.
  To the roots of the mountains I sank down;
  the earth beneath barred me in forever.
But you, Lord my God,
  brought my life up from the pit.
  "When my life was ebbing away,
  I remembered you, Lord,
and my prayer rose to you,
  to your holy temple.
  "Those who cling to worthless idols
  turn away from God's love for them.
But I, with shouts of grateful praise,
  will sacrifice to you.
What I have vowed I will make good.
  I will say, 'Salvation comes from the Lord.'"
  And the Lord commanded the fish, and it vomited Jonah onto dry land.

Jonah Goes to Nineveh

Then the word of the Lord came to Jonah a second time: "Go to the great city of Nineveh and proclaim to it the message I give you."

Jonah obeyed the word of the Lord and went to Nineveh. Now Nineveh was a very large city; it took three days to go through it. Jonah began by going on a day's journey into the city, proclaiming, "Forty more days and Nineveh will be overthrown." The Ninevites believed God. A fast was proclaimed, and all of them, from the greatest to the least, put on sackcloth.

When Jonah's warning reached the king of Nineveh, he rose from his throne, took off his royal robes, covered himself with sackcloth, and sat down in the dust. [7] This is the proclamation he issued in Nineveh:

"By the decree of the king and his nobles:

Do not let people or animals, herds or flocks, taste anything; do not let them eat or drink. [8] But let people and animals be covered with sackcloth. Let everyone call urgently on God. Let them give up their evil ways and their violence. [9] Who knows? God may yet relent and with compassion turn from his fierce anger so that we will not perish."

When God saw what they did and how they turned from their evil ways, he relented and did not bring on them the destruction he had threatened.

Jonah's Anger at the Lord's Compassion

But to Jonah, this seemed very wrong, and he became angry. He prayed to the Lord, "Isn't this what I said, Lord, when I was still at home? That is what I tried to forestall by fleeing to Tarshish. I knew that you are a gracious and compassionate God, slow to anger and abounding in love, a God who relents from sending calamity. Now, Lord, take away my life, for it is better for me to die than to live."

But the Lord replied, "Is it right for you to be angry?"

Jonah had gone out and sat down at a place east of the city. There he made himself a shelter, sat in its shade, and waited to see what would happen to the city.   Then the Lord God provided a leafy plant and made it grow up over Jonah to give shade for his head to ease his discomfort, and Jonah was very happy about the plant.   But at dawn the next day God provided a worm, which chewed the plant so that it withered.   When the sun rose, God provided a scorching east wind, and the sun blazed on Jonah's head so that he grew faint. He wanted to die, and said, "It would be better for me to die than to live."

But God said to Jonah, "Is it right for you to be angry about the plant?"

"It is," he said. "And I'm so angry I wish I were dead."

But the Lord said, "You have been concerned about this plant, though you did not tend it or make it grow. It sprang up overnight and died overnight. And should I not have concern for the great city of Nineveh, in which there are more than a hundred and twenty

thousand people who cannot tell their right hand from their left—and also many animals?"

In the end, Jonah gets upset with the Lord because the city of Nineveh didn't receive the judgment God warned them about. Who knows? He might have even been upset because they didn't receive the harsh judgment like he got for not listening! I feel sometimes those of us that are serving the Lord with such weighty mantles often forget the truth of who God is. God says, "I am that I am." It's not I am because anyone else said so. God is not God because Billy Graham said so. His ways are not our ways. He is not alive or moving because we said that He could. He is God. We don't have any say in His decisions and more times than not; we cannot change His mind on a matter.

Of all the prophets, kings, and examples of God's heart that are in the Bible, no one could persuade God to change His mind on what He wanted to do without complete repentance. Lot pleaded with God's angels to save Sodom and Gomorrah (**Genesis 19**) and was unable to find holiness in a town meant for total annihilation. Hosea pleads for Israel's repentance. (**Hosea 1-12**) King Hezekiah pleads for his life and his city, but God only grants him 15 more years and God clearly tells him that He will only save the city for His sake and for His loyal servant David. (**2 Kings 20**)

Ever since Christ died on the cross for our sins it appears we have lost the respect that God demands. Even as Christians we have gotten relaxed in our convictions. First-world problems have spoiled us and our children. Even since my childhood, I have seen such an increase in disrespect for things that used to motivate the goodness in people. Our elders, our government, our laws, our freedoms, our rights, our churches have all been trampled on. We have allowed the evil in the world to raise its ugly head and run a muck. God tells us that if we spare the rod then we spoil the child. (**Proverbs 13:24: Whoever spares the rod hates their children, but the one who loves their children is careful to discipline them.**) I feel that the rod wasn't referring to just to the disciplining of our children during times of disobedience but to the act of discipline altogether. That if we weren't diligently paying attention to the evil that was all around us and controlling the flesh inside us then we could lose all that we love. As parents, we can never take our eyes off our children when we are out in public. We have to have an ever-watchful eye on them to keep them safe and away from danger. We have to be a responsible parents keeping up with where they are, who is around them, what is around them, and what their needs are. As they get older the stress of the ordeal decreases because they begin to learn how to be responsible for themselves and to do the things that you used to do for them.

The word discipline means to practice the training of people to obey rules or a code of behavior. The act of using punishment to correct disobedience. I love how the definition says to train people. I believe that as new believers God is training us to watch after our spiritual newborn soul. We have to watch out for people and their intentions. We have to make sure that the information that is given to us is aligned with God's Word. We have to listen to our Heavenly Father to teach us how to react to others. We need to listen to Him on how we are supposed to care for our soul in delicate situations with our family members or friends who don't believe the same way we do. Like a child, we have to rely on God to show us the way through this thing called life. As we get older, I feel that God's watchful hands relax a little away from us as He gives us the freedom to grow. He doesn't have to stand over us as long as we have shown Him that we can be responsible and faithful Christians. We can listen to His Word and His voice to be able to walk in the world on our own.

Unfortunately, the next stages in our walk with the Lord look and sound a lot like our indignant teenage years. We learn a little bit and we all of a sudden think we know everything. We start walking quicker without watching our step. Speaking louder than we should. Messing around in adult conversations like we understand what is going on. Treating other newborn Christians like they can't handle anything and trying to shut them out of our newfound freedoms like a younger sibling who you don't want to hang around with anymore. Almost running right out into traffic unaware of the dangers that are actually around every corner now. Not realizing that every evil spirit has a bull's eye on us. Ready to attack us at any given moment. We take on the world like it has no idea of the strength we have acquired in our holster and it better not test our abilities in any way.

When all of a sudden as our loving parent, God sees all and knows all. Like the loving Father He is He stands back and tries to tell us those friends aren't right for us. He knows that one of them is a drug dealer and is addicted to alcohol. He doesn't want you to go to that party because there will be too many people on the balcony outside and it will fall. Kids will die. He tries to convince us the dark alley isn't a safe place for us to be ministering. He takes our car keys away from us because we don't see the dangers on the road during the hailstorm satan is firing on our loved ones and the hail will cause you to wreck and lose your legs. He grounds us in our job positions because if He would allow that promotion to go through it would put us in a position where a disgusting sexual addict would be your boss. He is screaming at you to listen to Him because He only wants you to be safe and He wants you to thrive in a better world than our parents did.

The enemy is always there trying to destroy your walk with the Father. He is there in the night plotting your downfall. Planning your demise. Pursuing to blow out your light and become useless to the Kingdom of God. As a Christian, you will never have freedom from those attacks. Never. The enemy never sleeps and he never stops trying to destroy you. But God tells us that we are never alone. As our loving Heavenly Father, He tells us how to move through life; protected, safe, and able to show others how to do the same. That He will always be with us during the walk. He will be there and He will give us the right prayers to pray through the guidance of the Holy Spirit. He will give us the weapons to use against any enemy that comes against us. He tells us how to fight the battles and how to defeat the enemy where he is at.

Isaiah 41:10: "Fear not, for I am with you; be not dismayed, for I am your God; I will strengthen you, I will help you, I will uphold you with my righteous right hand."

Psalm 23:4: "Even though I walk through the valley of the shadow of death, I will fear no evil, for you are with me; your ROD (your disciplines) and your staff, they comfort me." A staff is what a shepherd uses to tend to the sheep trying to wander away from the flock. It is a long carved piece of wood that has a long curved

"U" on the end that is used to come around the neck of a sheep and lead them back into the fold and protection of the flock. You see in the animal world animals who are singled out and left out alone are easy for predators to chase down and kill. But if the animals stay closer together they have a greater strength in larger numbers. Four hooves aren't scary to a predator. However, four thousand hooves can trample any enemy to their death.

Ephesians 6:10-18: "Finally, be strong in the Lord and in his mighty power. [11] Put on the full armor of God, so that you can take your stand against the devil's schemes. [12] For our struggle is not against flesh and blood, but against the rulers, against the authorities, against the powers of this dark world and against the spiritual forces of evil in the heavenly realms. [13] Therefore put on the full armor of God, so that when the day of evil comes, you may be able to stand your ground, and after you have done everything, to stand. [14] Stand firm then, with the belt of truth buckled around your waist, with the breastplate of righteousness in place, [15] and with your feet fitted with the readiness that comes from the gospel of peace. [16] In addition to all this, take up the shield of faith, with which you can extinguish all the flaming arrows of the evil one. [17] Take the helmet of salvation and the sword of the Spirit, which is the word of God.
[18] And pray in the Spirit on all occasions with all kinds of prayers and requests. With this in mind, be alert and always keep on praying for all the Lord's people."

So many times in scripture we see God instructs us to **just stand and to be still**. It has been a very long time (17 years to be exact) since my Heavenly Father told me to just stand and wait on Him. Seventeen years of waiting to be used. Seventeen years waiting to move and become part of His Kingdom leading others to the Lord. Seventeen years of hearing His Voice and His instructions and not being released to speak. Seventeen years of sitting in His Presence and soaking up His Love. Seventeen years of just standing still. After Seventeen years, I can finally say I now know why He says that so often to us. I always tell my kids that if they have trouble doing what they are trying to do, then to slow down and think it through. If it's not working the way you're trying to do it then look at it a different way. If you can't figure out a better way to say something then slow down and think before you speak. I wonder if God isn't answering our prayers the way we would want them to be answered because God is trying to protect us from something we do not see in our futures.

In my experience, the enemy has always been quick to move. He is always in a rush to have his way. Like an undisciplined toddler, he runs around throwing temper tantrums, screaming, yelling in frustration, throwing stuff around causing chaos and hurt. No one likes an undisciplined child who runs around in a restaurant acting like don't have good parents teaching them how to act. So as you see, God our Father in Heaven wants us to stand still and listen to His voice as He teaches us how to handle the situation. Let Him show us how to speak to the girl in your Chemistry class to see if she'd like to meet you at the movies for a date. Let Him show you how to talk to that unbeliever at work who had another church hurt him. Let Him show you how to tell others about Him. Let HIM show you HIS PURPOSE and WILL for your life here on Earth. Give Him the time He needs to show you how to get through this situation without hurt, pain, and conflict. Give Him the time to reveal His secrets to you.

Sit back and you will soon realize that there is an enemy in your midst there to cause you harm. Be still in the wilderness and let the enemy unveil his plan to harm you. Because that is exactly what will happen. He can't sit still and just be. He is envious of your Father's love for you and he wants to keep you from any blessing God has for you. Don't allow him to do what he wants in your life. He lost the right to your life when you asked God to come into your heart and to be your Lord and Savior.

Now some aren't quite ready to be mature in God's love yet. We get through the "teenager phase" of our walk with the Lord but we still can't manage to get to a place of true peace and reverence. Instead of allowing the Lord to teach you what He wants to teach you in the moment to overcome your troubles you allow the quickness of frustration, envy, fear, jealousy, pride, or anger to come in and ruin a foundation of good that God had laid before you. I have seen it happen in every church I have ever walked into. Instead of being still and allowing God to speak through the situation you get hurt and offended; storming out to find another church that will treat your daughter like the queen she is. Or to find a church that will let you be on the board because you gave them a large sum of money. Or you will find a church that has more able bodies to help your sound, children's, or youth ministry to flourish like you want it to. Instead of allowing God to teach you about the things HE needs to teach you before He can grow your church.

These days we are seeing more people who don't want their sins confronted or to be dealt with. They just want a happy, comfortable Sunday service that has nothing to do with actually growing in God's Word. They want to spend an hour by the coffee counter and talk for a while. Only to walk in just as worship ends and listen to a great word that just pumped up your good spirits till next week. Only to leave exactly forty-five minutes later just before noon and a possible alter call is made or before others can catch up with you to talk some more. So that you can get to a restaurant before the other church members do. You don't feel called to help out anywhere in the church. You don't feel like changing in any way because you're happy with the life God has given you and that's all you're there for. Right?

Wrong!

Your complacency has become a comfortable routine and no one is going to mess with that. Your bills are paid. Your car is clean and washed. Your kids are doing great. You are fifteen minutes early to church. Nothing can mess with your perfect life. Except you forgot...there's more to your story. God has a will for your life. He has a purpose for you to fulfill. He has wanted to see you grow up into a mature productive Christian who leads, helps, and guides others to Him. Even as I type, I can hear you scoff under your breath. You don't believe me? You truly don't believe God has a purpose for your life while you are here on Earth? Let me prove it to you.

Matthew 28:16-20:

"The Great Commission

Then the eleven disciples went to Galilee, to the mountain where Jesus had told them to go. When they saw Him, they worshiped Him; but some doubted. Then Jesus came to them and said, "All authority in heaven and on earth has been given to me. Therefore go and make disciples of all nations, baptizing them

in the name of the Father and of the Son and of the Holy Spirit, and teaching them to obey everything I have commanded you. And surely I am with you always, to the very end of the age."

Colossians 3:16: "Let the word of Christ dwell in you richly, teaching and admonishing one another in all wisdom, singing psalms and hymns and spiritual songs, with thankfulness in your hearts to God."

Mark 16:15-16: "And he said to them, "Go into all the world and proclaim the gospel to the whole creation. Whoever believes and is baptized will be saved, but whoever does not believe will be condemned."

James 5:19-20: "My brothers, if anyone among you wanders from the truth and someone brings him back, let him know that whoever brings back a sinner from his wandering will save his soul from death and will cover a multitude of sins."

Philippines 2:12-13: "Therefore, my beloved, as you have always obeyed, so now, not only as in my presence but much more in my absence, work out your own salvation with fear and trembling, for it is God who works in you, both to will and to work for his good pleasure."

1 Peter 4:10-11: "As each has received a gift, use it to serve one another, as good stewards of God's varied grace: whoever speaks, as one who speaks oracles of God; whoever serves, as one who serves by the strength that God supplies—in order that in everything God may be glorified through Jesus Christ. To him belong glory and dominion forever and ever. Amen."

Mark 10:45: " For even the Son of Man came not to be served but to serve, and to give His life as a ransom for many."

Even Christ's purpose was to serve others in His time in ministry. His Life was to show others how to love as God did. To show goodness and mercy despite the evil. It was to show others how to show their light to others who did not believe. His Purpose was to show others how to serve the Lord despite the pain of hanging from a cross. His ministry was to tell us serving the Lord can happen despite whatever you are going through.

In this chapter, I learned that God's rules were not given for us to fear His punishment but to realize they were there because He loves us so much. Like a parent, He is keeping bad things from hurting us and getting in our way. He wants us to be Holy and Righteous so that we can spend more time with Him. As I grow in His ways I know He can release me to be used in a greater way in the future. That I might serve Him in a greater capacity later down the road. Were there any other revelations God gave you in this chapter?

_____

_____

_____

_____

_____

_____

_____

_____

_____

_____

_____

_____

Please pray with me:

Dear Heavenly Father,

Thank you for your love, mercy, and grace. Thank you for your protection when I wanted to move and you kept me from harm. Be with me Lord and Direct my path in the future. Help me to hear your will as we walk forward. Bring forth reverence to your presence in my life and community. Guide my actions when I show others who you are. Be with me as I show others that they are loved by you. In Jesus' mighty name. Amen.

"The fear of the Lord is the beginning of wisdom; all those who

practice it have a good understanding. His praise endures forever!"
~Psalms 111:10

7

Chapter 7: Service

As a Christian, your walk with the Lord must continue to grow alongside other believers. The gifts that God has placed in us were given to correct and to edify His Church for a closer walk with Him. The church body was created by Christ and we are called to serve Him by serving others in His love, grace, and mercy. If this chapter can convey a main point, it is that you are serving a church body of believers not for a pastor's admiration or recognition. You are not serving the church for glory, money, recognition, praise, or accolades. The gifts that have been placed inside us are not for our entertainment. God's gifts are given to praise the Lord. If you do anything for the body of Christ and expect anything in return for it. Then you're doing it for the wrong reasons entirely.

Colossians 3:23-24: "Whatever you do, work heartily, as for the Lord and not for men, knowing that from the Lord you will receive the inheritance as your reward. You are serving the Lord Christ."

I have seen so many people fall away from God and away from their church for these very reasons. They work as hard as they can to do something to better the church or to help their ministry grow in numbers. They work night and day as hard as they can to get it to work. Then after a while, they don't see the growth they had imagined for God's ministry. They become upset because no one else will help them. Then they become bitter enough to go to leadership to complain. Then they quickly burn out...Every time! In my walk with God, the first lesson is always the hardest for people in ministry to learn. If your work for the Lord is actually for men and their praises then you're doing it for the wrong reason. In all things do it with excellence because He is always watching. He sees your heart. He knows your mind. If the fuel that is motivating you is operating off of high praises or esteemed worthiness of the pulpit then your engine will not carry you long enough to finish the job He has assigned. Just know this ahead of time that you, alone, are never enough to carry any ministry beyond your circle of friends or family. YOU ALONE.

Every ministry is a seed planted by God. You have to "water it", and "prune" the weeds out of the foundation to allow the nutrients to get to the plant. You have to tend to the plant and give it a safe place to grow. You have to prepare a fence around the plant to keep groundhogs, foxes, and deer from eating the roots. You have to build a trellis to hold the weight of the branches till they can hold themselves up. You have to make sure your seed has air, water, and sunlight. But most of all you need to give your plant time to grow.

If there was a helpful hint of advice that I could give any inspired ministry leader it is this. If God has placed a ministry on your heart and you would like to walk it out, then your first step is to talk to your head pastors. You would be operating in their church and God tells us to respect our leaders and elders. Your pastors didn't become who they are today without walking through some things on their own. Allow them to guide you and discipline you in this journey. They will be the ultimate resource for helpers, aides, curriculum, materials, and many other tools that you will need in your ministry. Most pastors are excited to hear about God growing their church and would love the chance to help you do what God has created you to do. To Share the Gospel too. However, if for some reason at this stage, the ministry is asked to hold off or not move forward, don't get upset with your church leadership. Don't leave your church because you're not received right away. Don't hop around to every church in town till someone lets you do God the way you want to represent Him. Just be still and stand. Allow God to strengthen you in your walk. Allow God to teach you how to move forward. Hold on to the things God is placing on your mind and heart. Write them down. Make them solid and sure. It may not be God's timing for you to move right now. Seek His Will and His Heart till you are released. Keep gathering materials. Keep getting excited about what God is doing. Keep talking to your pastors about your passion.

Talk to others in your church positively about what God is doing in your life. Share with other members about what God is saying and doing in you. More than likely God is moving on others too and there is nothing better than having a team to work with. As a matter of fact, it is my best advice to help you start this ministry in a healthy way after you have received your pastor's approval to move forward. Find other people to help you collaborate, work, and share the load of responsibilities that arise. For example, if you're starting a children's ministry in your church to help the children in your church to grow in the Lord and His Word, then you'll need a schedule of people who are willing to take your lessons and teach them every Sunday. Create a schedule of who will be taking care of the art, or craft section of your lesson. Who will be responsible for all the tasks you will be handling in your ministry? By having others with you on this walk then you will always have people to talk about the issues and the problems with. You will always have a group of reliable people who will always be praying for the ministry with you. You will always have someone to troubleshoot and help you in your walk. You'll always have people to pray to the Father for His guidance and wisdom.

There is nothing worse than feeling alone in your ministry. Because after you begin your work, your enemy, satan, will begin his work to tear you down. You will have whispers of doubt come into your mind and heart like never before. You'll have distractions at work that will keep you from getting anything done. You will have car troubles pop up right out of nowhere. You will have financial troubles, family troubles, and friend troubles...the enemy will not hesitate to use everything he can to stop you and keep you from your ministry. You'll look back at the horrors and troubles that you will come across and you will realize quickly that satan is the cause of it all. Having trusted fellow believers beside you during these troubles will enable you to overcome these fiery attacks quickly and with the least amount of destruction to your ministry. But please remember that you need to be a leader and a prayer warrior for your team and their family's as well. Covering them with prayer, resources, and tools to equip them on this journey. You need to make time to eat, play, and rejoice with your team. Not just work on Sunday morning to get things done. These are the people who are enabling the work of the father to reach others. They don't work for you, they work for the Lord, but they are looking to you to be their leader in their duties. They need to feel like they can talk to you, so make sure you're available and you're effectively communicating what you need them to do.

This leads me to say this important part. You are serving the Lord. He has called you to do great things. But do not forget you serve the Lord. You will need to make time in your busy schedule to talk with Him and make sure you are doing what He is asking you to do. Are you saying the correct things He wants you to say? Are you using the right songs in your praise and worship ministry? Are you making the right people a member of your team? Trust me God will always answer you. He will never leave you or forsake you in these important moments. If you are having trouble hearing Him then you need to quiet the distractions and remove yourself from a place that keeps you from hearing His voice.

God is always speaking to you. Always. If you can't hear Him it is because you aren't in a place where you want to, or can hear Him. If the posture of your heart isn't in a good place or you're committing sinful acts then more than likely God needs you to get right before He will move forward in your relationship.

John 8:47: "Whoever is of God hears the words of God. The reason why you do not hear them is that you are not of God."

To be honest, verses 39-47 are the whole truth in this matter. If there is something God sees or hears in your mind or heart that needs to be dealt with then His instructions and discernment will pause until you make it right. Your walk with God is a purifying journey to His sanctuary and peace.

John 12:26: "If anyone serves me, he must follow me; and where I am, there will my servant be also. If anyone serves me,

the Father will honor him."

John 2:11-22: "Therefore remember that at one time you Gentiles in the flesh called "the uncircumcision" by what is called the circumcision, which is made in the flesh by hands— remember that you were at that time separated from Christ, alienated from the commonwealth of Israel and strangers to the covenants of promise, having no hope and without God in the world. But now in Christ Jesus, you who once were far off have been brought near by the blood of Christ. For He himself is our peace, who has made us both one and has broken down in his flesh the dividing wall of hostility by abolishing the law of commandments expressed in ordinances, that he might create in himself one new man in place of the two, so making peace, and might reconcile us both to God in one body through the cross, thereby killing the hostility. And he came and preached peace to you who were far off and peace to those who were near. For through Him, we both have access in one Spirit to the Father. So then you are no longer strangers and aliens, but you are fellow citizens with the saints and members of the household of God, built on the foundation of the apostles and prophets, Christ Jesus himself being the cornerstone, in whom the whole structure, being joined together, grows into a holy temple in the Lord. In Him, you also are being built together into a dwelling place for God by the Spirit."

Joshua 24:15: "And if it is evil in your eyes to serve the Lord, choose this day whom you will serve, whether the gods your fathers served in the region beyond the River or the gods of the Amorites in whose land you dwell. But as for me and my house, we will serve the Lord."

Romans 6:16: "Do you not know that if you present yourselves to anyone as obedient slaves, you are slaves of the one whom you obey, either of sin, which leads to death, or of obedience, which leads to righteousness?"

We all are a slave to something whether we want to believe it or not. We work for good or for evil. However, these days there seems to be the collective thought that we serve only ourselves. I've heard people say, "We aren't on either side. That we just get up, go to work, and earn money to pay our bills. Maybe go on a vacation or two. I don't kill or do drugs. So I truly don't believe that there is a heaven or hell. Those were made-up fiction constructs to conform us to an obedient law-abiding society. I was born loving women or men and there is nothing wrong with that. I'm not hurting anyone. You do you. I'll do me. Don't try to inflict your commandments on me and my life…I'm old enough. I can do whatever I want to."

I have heard just about every excuse in the book. I've been called some pretty horrible things in my lifetime but none of them hurt me quite as much as the words of an unbeliever and their hatred spewed at me. As Christians, we must love the sinner but hate the sin. But how do you deal with an unrepentant, unbelieving sinner? The answer is that you can't. God asks us to plant the seed of truth in their hearts but to leave them until they are ready to hear it. We can pray and intercede to the Father for them. We can help them and care how they are. God tells us that we can do all that we can do but to stand. He doesn't tell us to argue for Him. He doesn't tell us to belittle them. He doesn't tell us to call them ugly things on Facebook and start arguments. He tells us to pull them aside and to tell them the truth in love but to allow the Holy Spirit to convict them.

We don't need to keep pushing. We don't need to be right. We don't need to do anything else for God. The only thing we need to do is be the example of peace and happiness that He has given us. We are to show others that having God in our life is the answer that they need to find out more about. If we have to tear someone down to show anyone that God is the right way then we've got the message all wrong. Christ came to show us that there is a better way. A better way to live. Free from our temptations to the things that kept us from being happy. Free from sin. Free from anger, hatred, jealousy, revenge, envy, rage, shame, hurt, pain, and fear.

Christ came and showed us there was a better way to help others let go of those things. He came to show us that all we had to do was lead them to Him and He would take those bondages from us and break all the sin's curses they had on us. Again, we don't have to do anything aside from showing them to Christ.

* * *

John 3:16: "For God so loved the world, that He gave His only Son, that whoever believes in Him should not perish but have eternal life. For God did not send His Son into the world to condemn the world, but in order that the world might be saved through Him."

Luke 19:10: "For the Son of Man came to seek and to save the lost."

Romans 10:9: "Because, if you confess with your mouth that Jesus is Lord and believe in your heart that God raised him from the dead, you will be saved."

1 Peter 4:8-9: "Above all, keep loving one another earnestly, since love covers a multitude of sins. Show hospitality to one another without grumbling."

Luke 8:11: "Now the parable is this: The seed is the word of God."

1 Peter 2:12: "Keep your conduct among the Gentiles honorable, so that when they speak against you as evildoers, they may see your good deeds and glorify God on the day of visitation."

~*~

Any mantle that lies upon your shoulders is another gift from the Father above. He has called you to a life of loving others out of their despair. A place that you have known all too well. For it was not long ago that you too were there. A place that kept you held captive and distracted till God the Father reached into your life and brushed the darkness off of you. Till someone who carried their mantle and God's light to your door and told you about a better way to overcome your battles. God tells us in **Romans 12:1-2: "I beseech you therefore, brethren, by the mercies of God, that you present your bodies a living sacrifice, holy, acceptable to God, *which is* your reasonable service. And do not be conformed to this world, but be transformed by the renewing of your mind, that you**

may prove what *is* that good and acceptable and perfect will of God."
He tells us that this is a reasonable act of worship. I looked up the
definition of the word reasonable. It is an adjective and it means it *is as
much as is appropriate or fair, moderate.*

So when God tells us to go into all of the world and
proclaim His good news and to share our testimony; our truths, He's
not telling us here in Romans to give more than we can. He's saying
give what is appropriate and the only way we are to know what He
feels is appropriate in any given situation is to follow His instructions.
His lead. Listen to His voice and allow Him to tell you what to say or
do. My best advice for any situation is to wait on Him. **2 Peter 3:9:
"The Lord is not slow to fulfill His promise as some count slowness,
but is patient toward you, not wishing that any should perish, but that
all should reach repentance."** God will never be hasty or rash to jump
into any situation too quickly. His desire is that all will come back to
Him. He is always on time and His will is always perfect. So we can
never go wrong waiting on Him. Just always remember, God will
never ask you to do or say something that doesn't agree with the
Word of God or the law.

God gives us instructions in **Romans 13:1-5: "Let every
person be subject to the governing authorities. For there is no
authority except from God, and those that exist have been instituted
by God. Therefore whoever resists the authorities resists what God
has appointed, and those who resist will incur judgment. For rulers
are not a terror to good conduct, but to bad. Would you have no fear
of the one who is in authority? Then do what is good, and you will
receive his approval, for he is God's servant for your good. But if you
do wrong, be afraid, for he does not bear the sword in vain. For he is
the servant of God, an avenger who carries out God's wrath on the
wrongdoer. Therefore one must be in subjection, not only to avoid
God's wrath but also for the sake of conscience."** So God will never
tell you to break the law or to hurt one another. So if you are hearing
those instructions you need to stop what you are doing and not act
upon it. Then you need to tell someone; a pastor or youth minister.

~*~

If you feel impatient and you just can't wait to jump in

and serve the Lord then you can never go wrong calling your pastor. A church requires so many helping hands to get things done. There is always children's ministry, youth ministry, sound ministry, altar ministry, cleaning, outside flower beds, bushes, and trees that need to be tended to. The list goes on and on…There is always a place to help out! However, let me tell you this. The moment you step out to serve the body of Christ, your life will never be the same. God will open and clear your eyes to so many things. You will just know in your heart people's true intentions. Things that used to be fine are no longer okay. Situations that never bothered you before will bother you now. The more you dig into God's Word the more you will see evil for what it really is.

The enemy will come out full force against you to stop your service. As I have said many times before, satan will never stop trying to push you off your path. The only answer is for you to dig even deeper into the Word, spend more time with other believers, and keep working for the Lord. After a while, you will start to see a pattern to satan's attacks in your life and you will become stronger in your defenses against them. Your first defense against the enemy will always be your scriptures. God tells us they are sharper than a two-edged sword.

2 John 2:6: "And this is love, that we walk according to his commandments; this is the commandment, just as you have heard from the beginning so that you should walk in it."

Philippians 2:3: "Do nothing from selfish ambition or conceit, but in humility count others more significant than yourselves."

Walking our journey in service to the Lord is one that can be taken lightly and should never be shuffled through in vain. Our service to the Lord cannot ever be done for ourselves. If there is any task that is completed for selfish gain, that is all you'll ever get from it. Service to the Lord is the most amazing gift I have ever come across. Your service to others will always strengthen and encourage your journey. **Proverbs 11:25: "Whoever brings blessing will be enriched, and one who waters will himself be watered."** Those who give will have blessings overflowing. Pressed down, shaken together, and running over. Everything you pour out into healing others. God will then heal you. Every hug will be returned. All your energy and well-planted in this world will be returned tenfold.

Hebrews 6:10-12: **"For God is not unjust so as to overlook your work and the love that you have shown for His name in serving the saints, as you still do. And we desire each one of you to show the same earnestness to have the full assurance of hope until the end, so that you may not be sluggish, but imitators of those who through faith and patience inherit the promises."** His promises of the good He has spoken over your life will never return void. He has promised us that the good work He has started will be completed in us. Our strength is in Him. Our perseverance is in Him. All that we are is because of Him. No one can take Him and our relationship with Him away from us.

As the days are approaching we are constantly being pulled in opposite and confusing directions. Mothers and fathers are demanded of like never before in human history. From sun up till sundown, we are constantly needed. Work, house, cars, family, vacations, yard work...it's never-ending. That's just a regular, normal individual. So many different things are needing constant attention. Unnecessary attention. Fathers pulled away from his family because he has to work more for more money. Mothers pulled away from their kids and home. Kids have more homework, schoolwork, and extracurricular activities just to keep them entertained. Heck, everyone is so busy taking care of themselves that they can't even take care of their chores at home. Women need nannies and cleaners to do everything for them. I have heard preachers blame the fathers. I have heard them blame the mothers. Well, I am blaming them both. They have put everything in front of their relationship with God. If their relationship with God was intact then we wouldn't be seeking approval from others the way we have been.

I have always been raised that there is a natural order to the priorities in our lives. Your priority is your relationship with God the Father. Everything that you do, say, and are should come from a close intimate relationship with Him. You can't pour out love if your cup is already empty. You can't give directions if you don't ask the leader where you're going. You can't have the strength to do the tasks that you need to do if you don't build up your soul while spending time with the Father. In the Bible, God tells us that there will be ten virgins with oil lamps. Five will be asleep and will run out of oil. The other five will be awake and they will be with the Father and they will get oil for their lamps. The parable is telling us to always be in a relationship with God the Father. It is the only way we can always be filled with oil to serve His will for our lives. It is the only way we will be ready for when Christ comes back and calls us by name. It is the only way He will know who we are. Is to have a relationship with Him before His return to us.

Matthew 25:1-46: "Then the kingdom of heaven shall be likened to ten virgins who took their lamps and went out to meet the bridegroom. ² Now five of them were wise, and five *were* foolish. ³ Those who *were* foolish took their lamps and took no oil with them, ⁴ but the wise took oil in their vessels with their lamps. ⁵ But while the bridegroom was delayed, they all slumbered and slept.

⁶ **"And at midnight a cry was *heard:* 'Behold, the bridegroom is coming; go out to meet him!' ⁷ Then all those virgins arose and trimmed their lamps. ⁸ And the foolish said to the wise, 'Give us *some* of your oil, for our lamps are going out.' ⁹ But the wise answered, saying, 'No, lest there should not be enough for us and you; but go rather to those who sell, and buy for yourselves.' ¹⁰ And while they went to buy, the bridegroom came, and those who were ready went in with him to the wedding; and the door was shut.**

¹¹ **"Afterward the other virgins came also, saying, 'Lord, Lord, open to us!' ¹² But He answered and said, 'Assuredly, I say to you, I do not know you.'**

¹³ **"Watch, therefore, for you know neither the day nor the hour in which the Son of Man is coming."**

Second, comes your relationship with your spouse. Openly communicating with each other, loving, sharing every detail of your lives together. Working together to take care of the home and all the responsibilities that come from building a life together. Taking care of all the chores, decisions, and workload. If either partner feels that they are the only one working towards a goal then any foundation that was built in any castle will start to break down. That stands for the children and instructing and raising them as well. Dad can't always be the disciplinarian and Mom can't always be the only one picking up toys and running drops offs or the picks ups for the kids. Sooner or later if left to these destructive ways, resentment and bitterness will grow into a huge problem. To start, continue to be the loving and tentative partner you're needed to be.

1 Peter 3:7: " Husbands, likewise, dwell with them with understanding, giving honor to the wife, as to the weaker vessel, and as being heirs together of the grace of life, that your prayers may not be hindered. There are many scriptures in the Bible about our relationship with each other as husband and wife. But I love how the writer says that husbands and wives are heirs together in this life. We are working together with the grace of the Lord so that our prayers will not be slowed down. How many of our household blessings seem to be blocked during the time great stress and anxiety are present between the husband and wife? Too many times to count! If you have found that you feel far away from the Lord, start by looking at your relationships at home. If something isn't well in your marriage then that is what you and God need to work on first before you can tend to anything else.

Third in your priorities are your children that live with you. I say the children that live with you because it's not always our decision on whether or not we have a relationship with a child or not. Previous exes or spouses can make one's relationship with their children extremely difficult. Do everything you can do to have the best relationship with your children. Always be the God-fearing, loving parent that God has created you to be. Pray for them. Tend to their needs. Foster a healthy relationship with them and the Lord. Being the best example of what a heavenly father or mother should be because they will grow up one day and you may be the only example of goodness in their lives. Be the parent that leads them to the Lord.

Your Fourth priority is your work. I know we need our careers to pay our bills but there always has to be a balance between them all. Work would never come before your safety and the well-being of your wife or children. However, we can't stay at home with the family and never go to work either. So as you see there has to be a balance between it all.

Your Fifth priority is your service to the church. Not to be confused with your number one priority, God.   Also not to be confused with your church attendance. Even if you serve the body of Christ, it is always important to have time to be a church member. You need time to worship, fellowship, and go to the altar just like every other church member needs. But in this section, I am talking about the time you volunteer work for your church. I'm talking about the spare time when you go into the church to mow the grass, tend to the parking lot, or check on problems. I have witnessed many families who have put the church before the time they invest in their spouses and it has hurt an individual's relationships all around them. If your children think you go to the church more than their ball games then this might foster bad feelings in them towards the church. If you go to mow the grass or seal the parking lot at the church during your daughter's ballet recital, she might be hostile towards the church because you're investing more time there than you are with them. God will never want you to hurt others, especially your family for Him.

Nothing in this life should pull you away from talking, fellowshipping, or worshiping God. Yet, God understands our love for our family. He tells us in the scriptures about Job, that he prayed and interceded for his children just in case they should happen to sin. (Job 1:1-4) God hears honorable requests. We need to keep the honor and integrity of our hearts pure and righteous. We cannot control what others may do or say but we can control how we react and what we say to those around us. However, in God, we have the strength to overcome all adversaries. Including ourselves.

Isaiah 40:28-31: "Have you not known? Have you not heard? The everlasting God, the Lord, The Creator of the ends of the earth, Neither faints nor is weary. His understanding is unsearchable. He gives power to the weak, And to those who have no might, He increases strength. Even the youths shall faint and be weary, And the young men shall utterly fall, But those who wait on the Lord Shall renew their strength; They shall mount up with wings like eagles, They shall run and not be weary, They shall walk and not faint.

In this chapter, I learned that our gifts are from God and are to be used for God's Glory. Despite the evil arrows that are coming at us. The lessons we have learned are given to us so that we can serve and teach the body of Christ in their journey with the Lord. Our gifts are to encourage, build up and lift up others. What Gifts has God revealed to you in this chapter and how can you use them to serve?

_____

_____

_____

_____

_____

_____

_____

_____

_____

_____

Where in your church body of believers could your gifts be used?

[ ] Cleaning Ministry   [ ] Altar Ministry

[ ] Ushers Ministry   [ ] Pastoral Ministry

[ ] Greeters Ministry   [ ] Sound Ministry

[ ] Children's Ministry   [ ] Streaming Ministry

[ ] Youth Ministry   [ ] Video & Photography Ministry

[ ] Security Ministry   [ ] Offering Ministry

[ ] Outreach Missions Ministry   [ ] Community Outreach Ministry

[ ] Other

* * *

Please pray this prayer with me:

Dear Lord,

I love you Lord and I believe it is your will for me to walk in the next phase of my journey with you. I wish to be used in your house to bring others into a fuller relationship with you. I feel like I could be best used in the _____ ministry. But Lord I wish to be used where ever our pastor needs and sees fit for me to be used. Please guide me and give me the strength to serve your house to the best of my ability. In Jesus' mighty name. Amen

"And let us not grow weary of doing good, for in due season we will reap; if we do not give up." ~ Galatians 6:9

8

Chapter 8: Strength

In every Christian's journey, they come across a mountain or struggle that appears to be impossible for them to get through or around and I am sure that every one of them has thought the same thought when they're reading the Bible. "How in the world did that person in the Bible overcome that mountain?" The tasks God has placed before us were never placed there because of who we are. He knows we are unable to overcome it on our own. If we could do it on our own then why would we need God? They were placed there because of who lives in us. In our strength, we are no one and we know it in our hearts and our minds. We do not have the power to do anything miraculous.

That's what makes watching movies so much fun. We see these incredible endeavors and adventures in different times and different universes and we are in awe of their courage and strength. These adventures like the story about Lucy, Susan, Edmund, and Peter went on in *The Lion, The Witch, and The Wardrobe by C. S. Lewis* are so magnificent and grand that we couldn't imagine living through them. Crossing paths of an adversary like the white witch and her ability to make everything freeze. If we faced her could we overcome her evil alone? Could we tear down her reign? Could we stop her from hurting so many innocent people? Then I think about the people in the Bible. People like Moses and Noah. Think about it. Moses was instructed by God to go to Egypt and tell the Pharaoh to let His, God's people go.

That would be like you or I walking up to the President of the United States and demanding...well anything. The President would laugh at us while escorting us out of the way. We have no power in ourselves to demand anything of anyone. Could you imagine Moses' thoughts when God asked him to do that? He was the exiled grandson of the Pharaoh. The Pharaoh tried to have Moses killed because he had killed an Egyptian. Moses fled Egypt, as a murderer. A man without a family for support. Without a community to help him. I could imagine Moses fled more than just the loss of his social or economic labels. I would imagine he is just like the rest of us. He was fleeing the image of what the world says we are. What we think we are. Because whether we like to or not the things of this world affect our self-image greatly.

Look all around us and we are told we have to look a certain way. Speak a certain way. Act a certain way. All in the name of social acceptance. Heck. In this day and age, we're told we have to accept everyone just as they are regardless of their social, economic, or financial status. It's either all or nothing, right? Everyone gets a trophy for getting up out of bed or no one gets a trophy at all. When in all reality everyone loses. By not rewarding the exceptional in their specialty or their field it then removes the spectrum of what one could ever hope to achieve. When we look up to the people who have made their field great it gives us hope to keep pushing towards said greatness for ourselves. We see that they did it and we feel that we have hope that we can too. It gives us a goal to work towards. If you take away the goal it takes the journey away altogether. It's like you're telling us there is nothing worth achieving. That being great no longer matters but it does.

Spending hours in a gym practicing a basketball shot till it's perfected. It matters. Practicing your shot gets you closer to greatness. Continuing research till you find the cure for brain cancer. It matters. Continuing your research may mean we are another step closer to curing a horrible disease. We are closer to healing another child. Working hard and late hours to pay your family's bills. It matters. To your family, it means the world to them. They need your hard work and love. It matters more than ever but don't forget why you're doing it. Remember why you started this journey to begin with. Are you doing it for good? Are you doing it to help others? Is your energy that you're spending on restoration or is it tearing something down? Are you doing it for love or anger? Joy or grief? Peace or war? Or is it in revenge? To hurt? In hatred? To glorify self? To promote yourself? I guess a better question would be who are you doing it for? Who gets the praise when you complete your task? Who gets the praise if you give up on your passions?

Could you imagine Noah's everyday life? Getting up every day-- living with the laughter and ridicule that he had to endure from others because of what he heard the Lord tell him? Knowing that the Lord was so upset with people for their evil hearts that no one was worth saving. No one was found worthy except Noah and his family. The Bible says that God found Noah to be righteous in his generation. You know things had to be pretty bad when hundreds of thousands of people aren't worthy to live. The Bible doesn't tell us of the evil in their hearts but I would be lying if I felt they were anything different than us today. I think it is probably scary for one to realize how true this is. The Bible's account says that the inclination of the thoughts of the human heart was only evil all the time. They had fallen so far away from God that their thoughts were motivated by evil.

I don't know about you but when I watch the news today all I hear and see is bad, horrible current events that have taken place. More loss, death, and tragedy than ever before. I turn on the television for my daughter to watch cartoons after breakfast for a little while and I have to mute the tv because I have to be careful which channel is heard or viewed before I get to the children's station. Even that label on TV channels is no longer a safe rating guide. There are children's television channels that I refuse to allow children in my home to watch.

Evil is running loose everywhere these days and is no longer hiding in the shadows. Musicians, actors, actresses, food or drink commercials, and even some products have all allowed their infrastructure to be corrupted by evil. All making claims to worship the devil. Openly telling you that they can do what they want, say what they want, and be who they want without any repercussions or judgment. Making it look like being evil is the new great thing to do and say. Let me remind you that this is nothing new. The devil has been professing his greatness since his fall from heaven a thousand years ago.

As these days are increasing it is through us that we will see another great move of the Lord in His Power again. As Christians, we have the strength through the blood of Christ that gives us the right to say no to evil. To say no to evil in our homes or our workplace. We can say no to evil attacking our loved ones and family. We can say no evil being in our children's schools and in their private times. We know evil leads to death. It has no other purpose. We know that evil always comes with a heavy cost. Like any problem, you think that you can start with just a small amount of darkness and sin in your life and it won't hurt you. Then before you know it, it has ruined your life, caused you to lose loved ones and family. You gave away all your money for it. You lost your house, crashed your car to get it. Gave your clothes and possessions away to trade for its power. You lost your honor, reputation, and character for more of it. Evil is not a distinguisher of persons. The devil does not care who it hurts or shames. He just wants to hurt others as much as he can. These temptations and sins are the mountains evil has placed in our way to keep us from being who God has called us to be.

So let me ask you again, who are you spending so much time and energy working for? God tells us we are always working for someone. Is it for good or for evil? Is it for God or the devil? Ever since you began this journey with the Lord He has been by your side. Helping you...when you would let Him. Guiding you...when you would listen. Teaching you...when you were willing to learn. Just like He was with Moses when he was a young baby and his mother stowed him away in a basket to save his life. God knew exactly who the Hebrew people would need to speak to Pharaoh to get His people set free. God knew that He would need someone special to talk to Pharaoh. Someone who would eventually listen to what was being said. Not just anyone could walk up and talk to Pharaoh. Not everyone could plead with his heart and get his attention. Most people probably wouldn't even be allowed past the gate. But God knew who it had to be. God knew and prepared the way for Moses to walk in His calling.

God knew who He created Moses to be. From the day Moses was born, God raised him, guided him, and gave him a favor when it was needed. Protection when he was in danger. God even gave him his own mother's milk when he was hungry after he was taken in by Pharaoh's daughter. God allowed Moses to be raised in the Egyptian king's home so he would know their ways and customs so when it was time Moses would know what to say at the right time. God gave him the words to speak. He gave him the staff to do God's miracles. God gave everything to Moses that was needed to be who God called Him to be. Not to be used for evil. But to be used for God's will. Just like I know He has made a way for your journey.

1 Corinthians 10:21-22: "You cannot drink the cup of the Lord and the cup of demons. You cannot partake of the table of the Lord and the table of demons. Shall we provoke the Lord to jealousy? Are we stronger than He?"

~*~

Strength...such a mysterious word. By definition, it is only a noun used to describe someone's physical ability to do something or to describe whether someone is strong enough to overcome a task. By the world's definition, it is to measure one's physical strength. But God takes it so much further. For Samson, there was no one physically stronger than him. However, Samson was no match for Delilah and her ability to bait him into her bed. He was weak. King David, was a man after God's own heart. He was strong. He commanded King's armies to battle for the Lord, but in God's eyes even he had weak points in his reign.

I feel like we wouldn't be doing David and his story any justice if we left out how he grew up with older and stronger brothers than he. His father dismissed him many times in his life. Including the time the prophet Samuel came to the house. Samuel knew God's replacement king was living there and asked that all of Jesse's sons be brought out to him. David was out tending to the sheep and Jesse didn't feel he was worth mentioning to Samuel. Samuel knew someone was missing and asked Jesse if there were any more sons. All seven of Jesse's other sons had passed before Samuel and none of them were what God was looking for. Samuel even tells Jesse that not just the physical characteristics are what God looks for when choosing a king. It was all about the heart. David carried God's heart.

With God, it is always about your heart. When Paul is

writing us in Philippians and he is telling his friends that they do not need to worry about him because he has been through the low points and he's been through the highs. He has seen it good and he has seen it bad. He has seen what all seasons look like and there is nothing to worry about. With God, he can do all things because his strength is in God. Paul knows that in his own power, he is powerless. That when the struggle was hard and there was no way to overcome that obstacle the only conclusion was to give it to God and let Him move the mountain.

I have been a Christian most of my life and have read that specific scripture at least a hundred times and for that moment it was powerful and needed. It wasn't until today when I needed to know more about what Paul was intending to say that I pulled back and read the whole section. I really felt that I understood what Paul was trying to say from his heart. If for whatever reason the scripture isn't speaking or answering your questions then maybe you need to dig a little deeper like I did. Instead of just reading one scripture, read what was happening before and after the scripture. Read the whole chapter if you need to. All of God's words are powerful but nothing brings God's words into a powerful revelation in ourselves like the whole story.

Philippians 4:1-3: "I can do all things through Him who strengthens me."

As every Christian walks through their journey, we learn early that there is clearly another force against us. It gets in our way. Whether it's mental, physical, or even spiritual. It is there in between us and the path the Lord has laid out for us to walk through. When we become Christian we find that the opposition becomes easier to see but harder to get around. It's almost like our eyes had been covered our whole lives and all of a sudden they are now clear. We can see that evil is there and we know its purpose but it is still in our way. No matter how we war against it, it won't let us through to where we want to be. That is where God and His Word are key in our journey. In Him, we have the way through the mountain that is in front of us. In His Scriptures, we have the key to overcome and defeat this obstacle. God's Word is the only way to the truth that we can use to overcome the evil that is standing in our way.

No matter the barrier that has erected itself in front of us, God's Living Word will always be the way through that wall. If you wake up in the morning and you feel like you can't do anything right. Then go to God's Word and seek out the truth in the matter. If you have a hard decision about where to go to start your career and you don't know which path is the right one for you. Then go to God's Word and let Him direct your path. Having difficulty with a disobedient child and you don't know what to do. Then go to God's Word and let Him tell you how to handle the situation. Listen for God to speak to you about what you need to do. He will always tell you the right way to go. Always. He has never failed me.

Psalms 119:105: "Your word is a lamp to my feet and a light to my path."

John 17:17: "Sanctify them in the truth; your word is truth."

God's Word is the only living truth that we should apply to our lives. It never changes. Its only intention is to tear down evil and lift up God in our lives. It is the only steady foundation that can be built upon and will never fail us. His Word will build us up in the strength of God's love. If someone implies the Bible is to be used to hurt others then you need to go to God's Word and read it for yourself. Because God will never hurt us, leave us or forsake us. He promises us that in His Word. If God is asking you to change then it is always for the better. If He is asking you not to sin then it is for your good. If He is asking you to stop something then it is to keep you from harm. Living in His truth we can build a stable house that can never be knocked down. A fortified life built out of God's love. A life the world can no longer tear down. It can't be torn down because we know and feel its truth in our hearts and mind. It's a life we no longer have to defend, justify, or fight for.

To encourage one's self in the Lord means to sit with Him. Sitting in His Presence while we worship will melt away any attack that may come against us. Being with God during our prayer time will strengthen your mind, body, and soul in ways we would never expect. Just like that we are revived, restored, and rejoicing in life again. A small amount of time in His Presence and we can move forward with an energy we didn't even know we had. Our flesh is renewed and our mind is now clear. Spending time with our Lord and Savior can do wonders for the heart and mind. I believe that any great person moving with the Lord has spent a great deal of time with Him. Learning about Him. Studying His heart and how He thinks. Trying to understand His intent or meanings. Talking with Him and hearing Him speak on a subject is the only way we can ever have a close intimate relationship with Him or anyone for that matter.

Look at one of God's greatest generals in the faith; Smith Wigglesworth. An evangelist who won souls for the Lord in the 1890s. He and his wife, Polly preached the gospel, laid hands on the sick, and gave altar calls in Yorkshire England. He was known for his aggressive nature when he laid hands on the sick and his anger toward evil, sickness, and disease. Smith was often confronted about his aggressive demeanor during his meetings. During the 1920s Smith's plumbing business increased during a rough, harsh winter and he spent more time concentrating on his company instead of spending his time with God. Because of this deficit, Smith became more controlling and angry. One cold, wintry night Smith demanded that Polly stay at home and make him dinner instead of going to her prayer meeting. Despite Smith's backsliding Polly kept the course and kept going after the move of God without Smith. She continued her relationship; walking with God and listening to Him speak to her life. So when Smith demanded that he was her master and to stay at home she lovingly smiled at him and corrected him. "You are my husband but Christ is my master. I am going to church, Smith." She walked out the door and went to church.

In his anger, Smith turned the lock and locked Polly out in the cold night. Despite his fit, Polly came home, wrapped up in her coat, and fell asleep on the doorstep. In the morning Smith went to the door unlocked it and allowed Polly to come inside. She brushed off the snow and smiled lovingly at him again and asked him what he wanted for breakfast. It was at that moment God broke Smith Wigglesworth. The love she radiated to Smith could have only come from having a relationship with the true power of love. She had a relationship with God and it showed in her reaction to Smith in his anger. It was after that event that Smith was so ashamed and moved by her love that Smith locked himself in a room for ten days. Moved to repentance Smith knew it was time for him to go to His closet and spend time with God.

After his time in the room with God, it was said, he was a changed man. Never provoked to anger ever again. His fits of rage and depths of aggression were forever gone. The ten days Smith spent in the room locked in with God forever changed who he was as a man, as a husband, as a healer, and as a minister. Because of Smith Wigglesworth and his passion for the Lord, many have attributed his life to the reason many others have gone on into ministry. To quote Smith best, "The blood of Jesus Christ and His mighty name are an antidote to all the subtle seeds of unbelief that satan would sow into your minds." *Ever Increasing Faith.* We have everything we need to take down satan, just by speaking Jesus' name. So what could God do in our lives if we built our strength up in Him?

No one knows the struggle of being strong and weak any better than a paralyzed 17-year-old young woman. In 1967, Joni Eareckson dove into a shallow part of the Chesapeake Bay that forever changed her life. Paralyzed from the neck down Joni embarked on a lifelong mission trip through loss, depression, and a life of ongoing struggles that come with being in a wheelchair. In Joni's story, she is faced with the daily will to not carry on and to give up but she is always constantly reminded of God's strength through her faith. Leaning on Him every chance she can get to pull her out of the misery and despair her situation has placed her in. When she is too weak to move forward He holds her till she is ready. As an Advocate for the American Disabled, Joni presses on with the task God gave her of leading those in her ministry towards the heavenly Father through their disabilities and daily struggles.

Look at another in his walk with God. A self-promoted atheist. A man of science and wisdom. In his reasoning set out on a quest to disprove God's very existence. C. S. Lewis was a well-known author and writer but it wasn't till his endeavors to find God that God inspired his greatest creation. ***The Chronicles of Narnia: The Lion, the Witch, and the Wardrobe.*** A child-like tale of the story of good versus evil and war for your soul. However, Clive Staples Lewis' journey was one he took alone. One journey like so many of us have taken as well. All the proof he could gather against God but in the quiet parts of C. S.'s mind God won his heart. He denied God and God pursued him relentlessly. Speaking to His heart and mind; giving him the proof that God was undeniably real. It was in the secret place that God wins us all. It is through people we are introduced to Him but in the deepest parts of our spirit, we are drawn to Him. We are drawn into a deeper relationship with His heart and His Love. It is in His strength we are renewed and inspired to overcome the greatest chasms of the deep and through the wide.

The more time we spend with Him the more we can overcome. The deeper we push through the veil to get closer to Him then it is there we will find more of the peace we long after. It is in our time with Him that minds are changed, hearts are healed and bodies are rejuvenated. It is through God that we can do all these things. We can overcome depression, fear, sadness, heartaches, jealousy, anxiety, stress, rage, anger, hatred, and loneliness. All that we have to do is call on His name and ask Him to take it from us.

Every night while I was going through my divorce I was having terrible nightmares of my ex's treachery. The enemy was using my sadness and loneliness to terrorize me every night. It had gotten so bad that I began to fear going to sleep. I fought the sleep every night as long as I could, then I would pass out from exhaustion. One night the anxiety was too much for me to deal with any longer and through my tears, I called out to God and begged Him to take the anger, depression, sadness, and fear away from me. Within seconds my heart was relieved and my mind went to sleep. I awoke the next morning completely rested. I didn't have any nightmares or bad dreams. I just slept in the most restful sleep I had in years.

At first, I couldn't believe that God had answered my prayers. Now looking back I realize that I had allowed the enemy to come back in and steal God's victory away from me. In that moment of hesitation, I had given the enemy permission to take away the peace God had given me. So the next night when the fear started again I claimed my peace through the trust I was giving God over my life. So this time I asked God to take from me the fear and anxiety again. He did. His faithfulness is always on time and loyal. He will always answer you in some way. He might not always answer you with the request that you think or want but He will always give you what you need. His answer will always be for you to trust in Him. In your weakness...trust in Him. In your bill pile that is up to your neck... trust in Him. When you're terrified and without hope...trust in Him. You see God says we can do all things through HIM who gives us our strength. The key here is learning to TRUST HIM with everything in your life.

In this chapter, I learned about how to go to God to receive more of His Strength in my life to overcome the mountains and evil that have erected themselves in front of me. I have learned that God is looking at the pureness of my heart. That my intentions are to be used for good and not evil. As we read the scriptures in this chapter, did God reveal any new truths to you about His will and the strength of His Love that can be used in your life?

_____
_____
_____
_____
_____
_____
_____
_____
_____
_____

Are there times in your day that could be better used to get closer to God through Worship and Prayer? What times do you plan on giving to the Lord in your future?

_____
_____
_____
_____
_____
_____
_____
_____

Let us Pray to Him now:

* * *

Dear Lord,

We are so thankful for your love. It continues to teach us to overcome our mountains through your strength and in your time. Encourage me, Lord, to set apart time in my day to sit alone with you. To rest in your arms. To take your peace and stillness in my heart and mind. Guide me around this mountain that the enemy has erected to stand in my way. Please place people in my life that can support our time together and bring others into my life to help me bring these truths into my reality. In Jesus' mighty name. Amen

"But the Lord is faithful. He will establish you and guard you against the evil one."
~ 2 Thessalonians 3:3

9

Chapter 9: Trusting in Him

One of the lessons I had to learn was trusting in the Lord when nothing made sense to my natural mind. Right after my husband had left me after thirteen years of marriage I was left curled up on the floor of my living room calling out to God, "Why God!?!? What did I do to you? What did I ever do to deserve this?" I wanted Him to answer me. I wanted Him to tell me why He was allowing my husband to leave and abandon us. I followed after God and was a good girl most of my life. I went to church, listened to His Word, and served my community the best I could. Why was He allowing my ex-husband to become a cheater just like my wrenched father had been most of my life? I was calling out to Him and as clear as day He answered me. He said, "Because you didn't follow after me first in your life." At that time I felt in my heart and saw in my mind what He was talking about. Everything we had done as a couple was for ourselves. We weren't helping others. I saw the sins of my ex's heart. I saw how horrible God felt about his "helping others." I heard God telling my heart how I just sat by and let my ex ruin our lives. How I had allowed him to become the man he had become. How I had not confronted his sins and turned him from those ways. By not telling him he was doing wrong I had allowed him to become the man that was breaking his promises and hurting our family.

That was hard for me to hear that from God because I was always under the belief that each person was responsible for their own walk with God. I was only responsible for myself and my actions and no one else's. So why was my ex's direction and relationship with God my fault? I couldn't understand it. My mind and heart couldn't wrap itself around it at all. As I have said many times, I have to go to scripture to understand more about God's heart when He speaks to me. It was then I found many verses telling me how to correct a sinner but there was one scripture that struck me to my core in regards to my ex being my responsibility.

2 Thessalonians 3:15 NKJV: " Yet do not count him as an enemy, but admonish him as a brother." Maybe it was in correlation with all the other scriptures that I had read that day, but this one struck me hard when God was correcting me. I began to cry even more asking God what was I to do now. I remember asking Him, "What do I do now? I just put Taylor to sleep and gave her the last of the milk to go to sleep. I have no money to even buy groceries for us to eat. What shall I do now?" He quickly answered, "Just Trust Me. I will provide."

A few seconds later I heard knocking at my back door. I jumped up, dried my eyes, and went to the back door to answer it. Not sure what I was going to find because no one knew my ex and I had just separated and I hadn't told anyone yet. Not even my family. Too ashamed to tell them that they were right. Too prideful because many years before they told me he was bad for me and to get away from him. They had tried to tell me he was going to do me wrong. They tried to keep me from him and I ran even closer to him. Saying they didn't know what they were talking about. They were wrong and they just couldn't see his heart. How could I tell them he proved them right and was a cheater who had taken all our money and savings...

Sorry, I'm getting away from the point of my story. Back to the back door...I opened the door and there stood my neighbor in her bathrobe. It was eleven o'clock at night and there she was standing at my back door. I welcomed her in. At first, I thought she was needing help with something but she got right to her point. Earlier that day her husband was praying during his devotional time with the Lord and God told him to come down to my house and give me two hundred dollars. She said that he thought he wasn't hearing God correctly and he shrugged it off. All day long God spoke to him again and again to bring me the money. He ignored God all day. But here it was at eleven o'clock at night and he was exhausted and God wouldn't let him go to sleep until he had done what God wanted him to do. So here she was at my door obeying the voice of the Lord. She handed me a check for two hundred dollars.

You see God had begun early that morning speaking to my neighbor. God already knew at eleven o'clock at night I would be on my knees asking God for help. God knew at that time His answer would be needed. In His timing, God's provision would be the answer I needed to hear Him on a deeper level. To have a more intimate relationship with Him. He knew I wasn't following after Him and now was the time for me to come out of the grave clothes and live again. God didn't do this to my marriage but He was there in the lowest points to pick up the broken pieces of the wreckage. He didn't do this to me and my ex. My ex's sin did this to us. So in my rubble, I stood up and knew God was going to take care of me. Although this was just the beginning of the lesson, I now knew I had to trust in God through the end of this relationship.

What began that night was a 12-year custody battle for my daughter that I could have never made it through without God and my close family. A custody battle that still to this day makes no sense to me but here I am still standing on God's promises and His Word to just stand, to wait on Him to do the work to the end. I could have a hundred more chapters to write about all the ugly, horrible things I have endured from the enemy but I will save us the time and negativity of it all to say this. I lost the custody battle for my daughter. I can't tell you how or why because I don't even know myself. But I will tell you this, God has not let me down. He has always provided for me. He has always directed me and He has always shown me His Love through it all. I had to let the battle with my ex go and I have to trust God with her life now.

For whatever reason God didn't part the Red Seas for me and my daughter to escape the monster that held us captive. Well, I got away but my daughter did not. But I know she hears God's voice. She knows what He sounds like. She knows she can open her Bible and talk to Him freely. I have to trust in Him to guide her steps to freedom just like He has guided me through. I have my good days and my bad days. I have days when she is all I think about. Where the enemy has my brain on this constant loop de' loop reel of whatta, coulda, what should I have done better? Then there are days of rest where I only wonder a short while about her days. I know one day she will be able to sit down and tell me how she really feels. She'll be able to see her sister and tell her she loves her. One day we will get to be a part of her life again. She'll break free from the shackles that have kept her so scared all these years. God will give her the strength to tell others what she needs and wants. I have faith that one day will come. My trust is in Him.

I will be honest it's been a rough journey. I can't say that I have mastered it yet. Letting go. It's not easy letting go of the hurt and pain others have caused. I heard it was the body's way of protecting itself from future pain. But then again I have also heard our mind tends to forget the things that don't matter to the heart. So who knows why our minds react the way they do? I believe in my case it's always been to remind me not to make the same mistakes twice. After your mind and body get hurt a few times they start to remember the things that caused the pain. We learn to stay away from those things. A lot like stubbing your foot in the middle of the night. After a few times of searing foot pain, you will learn to walk on the other side of the hallway from that side table you keep hitting. So is the same with matters of the heart and memory. We remember the signs of the things that caused us so much hurt. We start feeling and seeing these signs pop up in our life and we are quick to push them far away from us. We learn to walk on the opposite side of the street from the cute-looking bad boy that we know will hurt us in the end. Or at least we think we have learned our lesson...

When in all reality we continue to hold onto the lessons like a security blanket. We hold onto them because we are so afraid that we will have to live with a repeat of our horrible past experiences. We begin to change the roads that we drive on. We hang out with different types of people. We go to extravagant lengths to not have to go through the pain again. The unfortunate dilemma begins to unfold. We walk in a blind state of fear unable to enjoy our journey or we will unintentionally step into the very situation we are trying to avoid. Either way, the experience doesn't help us avoid any more pain. It just brings a different type of pain. So how do we navigate through life with so many hurts? How can we ever trust anyone or anything we've been through ever again? We can only change our identities so many times before we run out of options.

That's where God's saving grace has come to save us. We don't have to be afraid of the future ahead of us because God tells us through Him our futures will be different. That if we trust in Him and allow Him to guide us then our lives will never be the same. Although I still don't have communication with my daughter, I have to trust that God is working all things together for our good. She's seventeen years old now and I am still learning to trust in Him for our future. I am constantly reminded every day that His loyalty is faithful and true. One day she will be encouraged to know us again and I know she will break free from the lies and hurt that has been done to her. I will remain strong and keep moving toward the Lord. I trust that she is too and one day we will be together again. But I will be the first to tell you that the daily waiting and trusting in Him to move has been difficult.

Although there are many scriptures of people in the Bible that trusted in God there was no one more loyal than a man by the name of Job. At the very beginning of this book, God tells us there was a conversation between God and satan. He accuses God of helping His people and therefore the people's faithfulness to the Lord couldn't be true. He tells God that if He would remove His covering and blessings then people would not be loyal. That we would turn from God and curse Him. But God says that there was one man who was righteous and upright. God says Job would shun evil and would not curse the Lord. The only restriction the devil had was he could not touch or affect Job's health. He could do anything to his life but physically hurt him. So Job's testing began. The devil begins to take everything away from Job. His home and farms. His cattle, his livestock, his wineries, his vegetation...and if that wasn't enough satan even kills all Job's children. Job's friends abandon him; claiming he had done something against the Lord. For what other reason would he be so dammed? Job's wife even left him and as she was walking out the door she told Job to curse God and die. Even through all of that Job still was faithful to the Lord. Job repented unto the Lord because he thought he had unknowingly done something wrong unto God. Job remained faithful to the Lord. Defending God to all who come against them.

It was then that satan accused God even further that it

was only because God protected his body that Job was loyal. That somehow Job was still strengthened by God's protection over him. So God gives satan access to torment his body but he could not kill him. So satan attacks Job's health. It was then that Job become covered in boils and rashes. As he scraped his sores with broken pieces of a pottery jar, Job's friends began to question his righteousness and integrity.

Now come on! Like it wasn't enough for Job to have to live through all he had lost. He now had to defend himself to the very people who were supposed to be there for him. The people he was the closest to are supposed to hold you up during adversity and struggle. Unfortunately not for Job. His friends weren't there to help him. They were there to try and figure out what Job had done to make God so mad at him. Now you know that had to be the worst day you would have to live through. The very people who you thought were by your side. Who were there in times of hardship or trouble? They were there through thick or thin. Ride till you die type of brothers, Right? Only to find out they did not believe in you at all and were willing to abandon you because they thought you had done wrong in the eyes of God. I have wondered through ready this if Job's friends were as close to God as they thought they were. At the same time, they did not have the Holy Spirit yet to help them to discern the Lord's will like we do today. Unfortunately for Job.

As I said, Jesus Christ died on the cross and rose again three days later. He told us then that there would be another that came after Him and would be there to help guide us. (Acts 2:1-13) He was referencing the Holy Spirit. With the Holy Spirit's help and guidance, we can discern these acts of others. Don't believe me? Ever felt the sudden nudge in your heart to hold the door for a co-worker? Or the deep feeling inside to leave a place because it all of a sudden felt like a bad place? Only to find out later that something horrible had just gone down and you silently were thankful for the guidance? Those were acts of the Holy Spirit helping you and protecting you from evil. Although those spur-of-the-moment intuitions are great, there is so much more to learn and hear from Him. I feel like there is always more to gain from listening to the Holy Spirit than listening to the negative advice we could get from other sources.

I think that in this day and age, it is more important to

concentrate on listening to the Lord and His guidance than it is to listen to anyone else. God tells us that in the days ahead the enemy will turn the father against his son. Mother against daughter. Brother against brother. I think it's safe to say there is no one we can trust except for God, His Son, and the Holy Spirit. In my experiences, I can say if it doesn't line up with what God's Word tells us then we are to quickly disregard it and put it away from us. Again, we will know it by its fruit. If we are instructed to cause another pain, harm, or hurt. It would not line up with God's Word and we should dispose of it quickly. In the Old Testament, God gave Moses 10 Commandments for us to follow. But when Jesus fulfilled the prophecy and the law He simplified the commandments to two living rules.

The first commandment was to love the Lord thy God with all their mind, heart, and soul. The second commandment was to love your neighbor as yourself. Following those two commandments simplified all we are instructed by God to do. Despite all the world and other people have done to us, said about us, spoken over us, done to our children, stole from us, taken from us…Despite all that has been done to us we are asked to love. Just as He Loved us.

1 John 4:19-21: " We love because He first loved us. Whoever claims to love God yet hates a brother or sister is a liar. For whoever does not love their brother and sister, whom they have seen, cannot love God, whom they have not seen. And He has given us this command: Anyone who loves God must also love their brother and sister."

Despite what they have done to us we are called to love them. I know. I know. I can feel the hesitation in you from here. God calls us to love them but how in the world do I love someone who has done me so wrong? Right? I heard you and I know exactly how you feel. I rolled my eyes and crossed my arms when my sister in Christ told me the same thing regarding my ex and the troubles we were having. Lord knows I still have a knot in my throat just thinking about being nice to him if I were to see him in public. Under my breath, I'm still crossing to the other side of the street because I learned where my hurt and pain were coming from for so many years.

Romans 12:17-21: "Do not repay anyone evil for evil. Be careful to do what is right in the eyes of everyone. If it is possible, as far as it depends on you, live at peace with everyone. Do not take

revenge, my dear friends, but leave room for God's wrath, for it is written: "It is mine to avenge; I will repay," says the Lord. On the contrary: "If your enemy is hungry, feed him; if he is thirsty, give him something to drink. In doing this, you will heap burning coals on his head." Do not be overcome by evil, but overcome evil with good."

I just love how God knows us in our deepest inner souls, Right? In our anger, He knew we would want to lash out in our pain. He knew we would want revenge for the hurt they caused us. "Live in peace with everyone..." He says. Let Him have the revenge that they are due. He wants us to let Him deal with them and all we have to do is be good. Be honorable. Be righteous. Despite that, they are doing evil to be good to them. Show them how to be good even during the trials. Show them it is possible to be good even when others aren't. Tell nonbelievers that they are capable of good works despite the way they were raised to be. Trained to be. He tells us the only way we will ever overcome evil is to be good with good acts. With good words. With good motives in our hearts.

Posturing your heart to see His Face and to commune with Him in everything we do. That alone is hard to do daily. We need God to go to Wal-Mart these days! It seems that everywhere we turn we are attacked by evil. So I want to tell you how I learned to overcome the most hurtful of evils that have come against me.

First things first. There is evil everywhere we turn. From every crevice of every building to the cars on the street. Hurt and pain can come from far away but more than likely they will come from those who are the closest to us. Otherwise, would it hurt so much if it came from someone we didn't know? Nope. Betrayal only comes from those we trust. So we must always be on our guard to be mindful of our actions. We cannot always control others but we can control our own words, actions, and mindsets. Our first step is to always stay close to the Lord. We will always need God's eyes and ears to discern others' intentions. We wouldn't want to mistake someone's heart because we weren't seeing them through God's eyes. We don't want to push others away from God. We want to draw them closer.

The best way to see with God's eyes is to step away from the situation. Maybe not actually moving away physically but changing your point of view. I always imagine my soul coming out of my body and looking down at the situation from a higher point of view. You know, looking down upon what is going on. Hovering quietly above the moment and allowing God's eyes and ears to perceive the heart of the matter. Almost 99% of the time my next move is to do or say nothing that will escalate the hurt in that moment. That's what satan would want to have happen. He would love to use me for evil instead of good and I just refuse to allow him to use me to hurt others. So I have learned to stand quietly until my words can match God's heart. Sometimes it takes a while; a long while but it never fails. God shows me how to see things differently. When I pull my head and heart away from a heated moment I always ask God to show me what the devil is trying to accomplish in this event. I ask God to show me what information I am missing at this moment that is causing it to not make sense to me. Once I have diffused my own heart I can see what God wants me to see and hear what God wants me to hear. Getting us to a place where our hearts are pure.

Changing our hearts is almost as hard to overcome as changing our minds. If you can overcome the hurt of the past and teach both your mind and heart to trust God with your everything you will begin to see God move in your life like He never has before. Because when you allow God to guide your heart He will begin to order your steps, guide your hands and speak in His love language. It's in His Love language that you will see hurts healed, families restored, bodies healed, blind people will see again, and the lame will walk again. When you allow Christ to take over your heart you will begin to usher in His Presence into your life and into your home.

In this chapter, I learned how to trust God with the most important person in my life. My first daughter. I had to learn to let her go and allow God to watch over her and protect her when I couldn't. I also learned that through God's heart, I could see my situations from His Point of View instead of my own. Are there any areas that God has spoken to you about giving to Him?

_____

_____

_____

_____

_____

_____

_____

_____

Has God given you any new revelations on how you can learn to Trust in Him further?

_____

_____

_____

_____

_____

_____

_____

_____

Please pray this prayer with me:

Dear Lord,

There are several areas in my life that I have held very close to my heart. I have held them for so long and despite everything I do I can not seem to make any changes to the situation. Lord, I need your help and I need you to help me to let them go and take care of them for me. I release the anger, frustration, and negativity this situation has caused my life to you. Give me the peace and comfort of knowing that you can do anything. I am thankful for Your Grace as I learn to fully Trust in You with my everything. In Jesus' mighty name. Amen.

"And my God will supply every need of yours according to His riches in glory in Christ Jesus." ~ Philippians 4:19

10

Chapter 10: Ushering in His Presence

At this point in my life looks nothing like what I thought it was going to look like when I was done growing up. It's not at all what I wanted it to look like. Every struggle and every detail of my life has come down to this very last breath. Only truth remains to redeem what has been taken from me. No matter what I have been through in my lifetime, God was always there. God was always watching over me, providing for me, protecting me from harm, and keeping me on my path. No matter where I was or who I was with— He was always there for me.

When I was young, I always thought I was someone great. I just hadn't been discovered yet. The world was an adventure and I longed to explore all its possibilities. I imagined a grand youth life. Traveling and seeing the world and meeting lots of wonderful personalities. Maybe meeting my true love and then coming home to settle down. A beautiful family in a big farmhouse, with many rooms. Extra rooms to lend out a helping hand and to shelter others in need. Serving and giving back to my community and leading others to Christ and His great love. A big backyard and a pool with a sloping slide. The house is surrounded by tulips, roses, and lilies. A place for friends and family to come and visit and have a big cookout. A field of wildflowers and bluebonnets...

No one ever told me there wouldn't be enough time to do everything that I wanted to do in this life. There was no mention that my body wouldn't be able to climb a hill at forty-four. Or that I would no longer be able to go grocery shopping or stand at a counter to work. At forty-four my life stopped dead in its tracks and there was no hope of ever getting to be able to do the things I thought I was called to do. Fortunately for me, that's always how God has entertained my life.

Just when I had exhausted all the avenues that I thought I could walk through all my problems, God comes in and says, "Now please step out of my way and let me handle things." Most of my life that has been what my relationship with God has looked like. I, rushed in trying to quickly move mountains all on my own. Only for me to hit a hard unmovable wall and realize there was a better and easier way to do things if I would've just waited on God to show me how. If I would've just asked Him instead of struggling out there all alone. You would've found me sitting in a big mud puddle screaming in frustration, "Come on God! You couldn't have come in thirty minutes ago and shown me a better way to get over the mud puddle?"

Every time things don't go our way, we tend to think, "Why doesn't God love me? Why is He allowing them to do this to me? Why won't He stop the hurt? Where was God when I needed Him?" We quickly rush to blame Him for all our troubles. Never the one who God tells us is the troublemaker. Or better yet we never blame ourselves for the dumb decisions we just made that got us where we currently are. My ex and I were dating and we were arguing over my decision to pull away from him after a family vacation without him. His family's answer was we just needed to get to the church service on a Wednesday night special service meeting. At that meeting, God told me to walk away from him. To stop dating him and let God bring me to someone else He had created for me.

God even used my ex's sister to point out a man on the stage singing to God. I smiled and said no, that I was faithful to her brother. In my stubborn will, I ignored God and married the guy who would later cause so much grief in my heart and mind. Wasting 15 years of my life. Time, money, and taking my firstborn child from me out of pride and arrogance. Trying to justify that God's will for his life was to cheat on me with a better woman and let her raise our baby. You see the Holy Spirit was trying to save me a life of misery and heartache. Had I just listened to Him, I would have spared myself so much pain.

As Christians, we all are called to God the Father to have a relationship with Him and to witness to others according to His purpose for our life. Not all who are called will answer. However, those who hear the gospel and are compelled by the Holy Spirit to answer His call are a people set aside for His Glory. However, there are Christians who have been specifically chosen to interpret, share and evangelize the gospel. God has given us the Holy Spirit and He has given us spiritual gifts to aid us in seeing the world and other people for who it truly is. Although we no longer have Christ here with us to explain God's mysteries, we have the Holy Spirit here to guide us and direct us. He has also equipped us to pray, stand and fight the spiritual battles with us.

God has given His chosen people many different spiritual gifts for us to use to edify the body of God in the church. There is a gift of administration, teaching, exhortation, pastoring, evangelism, faith, discernment, giving, apostleship, leadership, serving, and mercy. God has given these gifts to build, edify, and serve the church. We are given all the different spiritual gifts. However, we may be operating in different ones at different times in our life. For example, we all are called to share the good news and share the gospel but not everyone was called to pastor a church and speak from the pulpit. Your "pulpit" might be on the street talking to the homeless or at a ball field speaking to athletes.

I understand you may want to know more about these spiritual gifts that God has given us and how they operate in our life but what I don't want is for you to get caught up in wanting more of God's Glory from God's people instead of going after God with all your heart. We want to focus on actually calling and ushering HIM closer to us. God tells us that darkness and light can dwell in the same place. Manufacturing what looks like God will only create more darkness and hurt more people. I came across a great website that has been a great tool in helping me learn more about these gifts in my own life. (www.spiritualgiftstest.com) Please go and check it out and make sure you dive deeper into the scriptures to hear what God is speaking to you about your gifts. Many scripture references will show you a revelation of each of the gifts in the Word. Remember drawing Him closer is our purpose in everything we do.

* * *

2 Peter 1:10: "Therefore, brethren, be even more diligent to make your call and election sure, for if you do these things you will never stumble; for so an entrance will be supplied to you abundantly into the everlasting kingdom of our Lord and Savior Jesus Christ."

When I was a new Christian I was so excited about Christ and what God was doing. After getting saved and baptized, our church youth group went to a week-long crusade for Christ in Pennsylvania. I was in awe of all that I was seeing and heard. I couldn't get enough! At that time, my family was attending a small Mennonite Church and until that crusade, I had never felt the Holy Spirit move like I was feeling in PA. In the worship and singing; God was moving and speaking in my mind and my heart. I couldn't believe what I was experiencing. When I came home I had to know more. We didn't have the internet and technology that we have now to learn. So I began to ask our church leaders and my youth pastors what it was I was feeling. Given that I was young it was explained to me in simple terms. "Oh, honey. That is God talking to you." Or "Well that is the Holy Spirit ministering to them." So as I grew up all I knew was that I wanted more of God in my life.

So as I got older and my observations of the things that I saw in the church changed with my age, I learned that the spiritual gifts we were given were being used in the church, and through the Holy Spirit, we could use these gifts to minister outside the church. However, did you see the spiritual gift called discernment? Yeah, I quickly learned that some were faking their gifts for attention or disruption. There is a strong warning in scripture about grieving the Holy Spirit.

Matthew 12:31-32: "Therefore I tell you, every sin and blasphemy will be forgiven people, but the blasphemy against the Spirit will not be forgiven. And whoever speaks a word against the Son of Man will be forgiven, but whoever speaks against the Holy Spirit will not be forgiven, either in this age or in the age to come."

The work that God wants to do in you for other people's guidance, healing, and growth is important to God and He wants to be represented truthfully. So those that represent Him need to be sure that they are doing so with the due diligence, respect, and honor that He deserves. His Presence requires nothing more and nothing less. So be sure to represent Him according to His Word. Honestly.

~ * ~

Before we get into talking about ushering in His Presence, let's look at the other times in our life when we are calling on Him to move. I don't know about you but most of the time when I am calling out and begging Him to act, it's when I am desperate. It's usually when I have done all that I know to do in a situation and I have no other ideas that will help me get through my dilemma. I call on Him when I am out of hope. When there's no one else I can call on. I am humbly before the Lord; calling out His name. But let's look to God's Word for others and the testimony of their need to call on God. Because when we come to the end of our ropes and there is nothing left to do. He is always there for us.

We all call on God for different things. Queen Esther called on God and fasted for her people to not be killed. Miriam, Moses' older sister, called on God to deliver Moses from the hands of death. Hannah prayed for the ability to have a child. Bartimeus cried to the Lord to be able to see again. Jonah cried out to God to be delivered from the mouth of a whale that had swallowed him. No matter why we are calling out to God, He promises us that He always hears our cries and that He will answer. We may not know how He will respond or how long it will take to respond but He will respond. His answer is always on its way.

Jeremiah 33:3: "Call to Me, and I will answer you and show you great and mighty things, which you do not know."

Look at the accounts of the interactions between the angel of God, Gabriel, and God's esteemed prophet, Daniel. God sent out His answer with Gabriel to Daniel the moment Daniel started to pray for Jerusalem. However, Gabriel and Daniel's answer was delayed because he was dealing with the Prince of Persia who was resisting him. He was delayed so long that one of the Chief Princes, Michael, had to come and release Gabriel to come to Daniel. So as you see God answers us but there are battles in the spirit realm that are keeping

God from getting His answers to us. (Please feel free to be a good Berean here and read about this for yourselves. Daniel 9, 10 & 11)

If you didn't know this, there is a war waged against God and His followers. The devil is doing everything in his power to keep God's will from drawing us closer to Him. We have our own free will, we have the will of others involved in our lives, and we have uninvolved people affecting our day, but then we also have spiritual and evil forces in our way of getting closer to God. With so much in our way, how can we get closer to God? What can we do to push away the darkness and run toward the light in God? Is it as simple as turning off the TV or putting down our phones? Do we just go outside and separate ourselves away from the craziness?

One of my study resources was **Revive Us Again: Biblical Principles for Revival Today** by Walter Kaiser. Kaiser points out nine characteristics of the revivals we find recorded in the Old Testament, which were originally listed by Wilbur Smith. I couldn't have said the conclusion of my research any better. But maybe added more details to every event, but I will let you go and read about these revivals for yourselves. Look at the First Awakening, The Second Awakening, The Third Awakening, The Revival at Azuza Street, and the life of John Wesley.

1. Most revivals were preceded by a time of deep spiritual decline and despair. For example, offering children as burnt offerings of the altar of Molech before the revival under King Hezekiah (**2 Chron. 29-31**).

2. Each of these revivals began in the heart of one of God's servants, who then became the instrument in God's hands to stir up the sleeping consciences of God's people. For example, Moses, Samuel, Elijah, Haggai, Josiah, Nehemiah, and others.

3. Every revival in the Old Testament rested solidly on a new and powerful proclamation of the Word of God. The most obvious example is the revival under King Josiah (**2 Chron. 34**).

4. Each revival was marked by a return to the genuine worship of Yahweh. "Wholehearted, genuine worship of the living God became the chief delight and one of the foremost desires of each person who was truly restored to spiritual vitality.

5. Revival resulted in the destruction of every idol that blocked the rightful acknowledgment of Yahweh as the only true and living God.

"This is true of every revival except the last two, which occurred after the exile when no idols were left in Judah."

6. There was a deep sense of sin and an overpowering desire to separate themselves from it and all its sponsoring causes. The work of revival is uniquely the work of the Holy Spirit. *(Not officiated by people.)*

7. In every revival in the Old Testament there was likewise a return to the offering of blood sacrifices. "Given such a heavy sense of sin, there must be as great a remedy, and that can only be met by the one and only sufficient sacrifice of the Paschal Lamb of God." *(I want to note here that the sacrifices that God has asked for have always been either the first fruits of a harvest or of an animal. NEVER A HUMAN SACRIFICE!)*

8. Old Testament revival resulted in the experience of a new sense of unbounded joy and exuberant gladness. "Nowhere is this seen more clearly than in that postexilic scene with Nehemiah and Ezra."

9. Each revival was followed by a time of great productivity and prosperity. "This is not the health, wealth, happiness, and success message that some are offering today. Rather it is the observation that the fortunes of the soil are intimately tied up with men and women and their spiritual success and failure."

Even if we look at the accounts of revival outside the scriptures throughout history there is always one common detail. There was a hunger for change that caused God's people to cut the sin out of their lives, a true repentance, and then a plea for God's mercy and grace that has humbled them to prayer, fasting, and worship. God's Word has brought forth many revivals. God requiring a change to better ourselves and our lives should move anyone to action. In the 1730s, John Wesley in his Oxford studies of the word with the Holy Club but it wasn't until he journeyed to the American Colonies that he witnessed such peace in a body of believers on a ship with him who were not afraid of the storm on the seas. John began a pursuit after this peace. He wanted this peace in his life and he wanted the change that only an intimate relationship with God could provide. He began to preach God's word in the fields. A message that the formal church prohibited. Speaking of God's love and God's grace was free for everyone. Not just the rich. The people's desperation for someone to love them and their need to be accepted required John and his brother to respond to their need to share God's word, peace, and love with others.

The hunger for more of God and a Pentecostal Revival, William Seymour traveled across many states and studied under many different preachers to further his education and knowledge of God in his lifetime. It wasn't till he reached Bonnie Brae's home in Los Angeles, California and a group of believers were praying, fasting, and listening to the word that Seymour experienced the breakthrough he'd longed for. Seymour and a small group of believers gathered to pray and read God's word. Seymour was preaching about Acts 1 and 2 and The Holy Spirit fell upon them and they began speaking in tongues. The crowds began to grow and cause a commotion. They moved their meetings to a larger building on Azuza Street to accommodate the crowds. For 3 years the revival on Azuza Street ministered God's presence to the people. Led by the Holy Spirit, William Seymour peacefully controlled the meetings and wouldn't allow anyone to steal God's Glory. He protected God's Presence in that place. He kept it Holy and reverent. Allowing only God to minister as He saw fit. True revival consists of our human hearts seeking more of God and our ability to sacrifice our will and our time to keep Him here.

~ * ~

As God has slowed my heart, my mind can't help but slow down as well. I'm not as young and as strong as I used to be. My heart attacks ensured a pace so slow I couldn't help but see the better things in life. So I see things with different eyes than I used to. It's almost as if God had to slow me down to get my full attention and teach me how to see things with His eyes and His heart. Slowing down has allowed me the time to reflect on God and what He's been trying to say in all the lessons that He has taught me and the conclusion has always been the same message. Both to me and the message He has spoken to millions of other people throughout time.

Colossians 3:12: "Put on then, as God's chosen ones, holy and beloved, compassionate hearts, kindness, humility, meekness, and patience,"

Ephesians 5:1: "Therefore be imitators of God, as beloved children."

* * *

If everything we have learned in our lifetime comes down to this one moment, then what is the final word? What is the message that God has been speaking since the beginning of time? He is saying that He wants us to purify ourselves to be holy and good. He wants us to put away our sinful desires and hurtful actions so that we can fellowship with Him again. He wants us to get to the place where we can show others His love and truth through our hearts honestly. He wants us to learn to forgive others and to learn to forgive ourselves for our sins. He wants us to repent of those sins so that we can serve Him and His Church with righteousness and truth. He wants us to be the example of Christ here on Earth. He wants us to be an ambassador in trusting Him and leading others to His Light. He wants to walk in the garden with us once again. He is saying we are HIS BELOVED. Everything He asks of us is because He loves us so much. Throughout scripture, you can read thousands of ways He is telling you that He is your Jehovah Jireh. Your Elohim. Your Yahweh Yireh. He is your Rapha.

1 John 4:11: "Beloved, if God so loved us, we also ought to love one another."

1 John 4:13-21: "By this, we know that we abide in Him and He in us, because He has given us of His Spirit. And we have seen and testify that the Father has sent His Son to be the Savior of the world. Whoever confesses that Jesus is the Son of God, God abides in him, and he in God. So we have come to know and to believe the love that God has for us. God is love, and whoever abides in love abides in God, and God abides in him. By this is love perfected with us, so that we may have confidence for the day of judgment, because as He is so also are we in this world."

Romans 8:38-39: " For I am convinced that neither death nor life, neither angels nor demons, neither the present nor the future, nor any powers, neither height nor depth, nor anything else in all creation, will be able to separate us from the love of God that is in Christ Jesus our Lord."

Your heavenly Father is all that you need. He has given

His everything for you. He has given His life for your freedom.

In the final chapter, we looked into our Christian Revival History. I learned so many details about how to draw God closer. In James 4:8 James himself tells us, **"Draw near to God and He will draw near to you. You sinners, purify your hearts, you double-minded."** We must purify our lives for us to draw nearer to Him. Cleansing our hearts and minds to go into the Presence of the Lord. I know while I was writing My Beloved the Holy Spirit constantly spoke to me about the things in each chapter that I had to lay down and give to Him. Did the Holy Spirit speak to you about some things in your life that you needed to lay at the cross? Journal your time with the Lord below.

_____

_____

_____

_____

_____

_____

_____

_____

_____

_____

_____

Dear Lord,

We have learned so much about our walk with you. We have learned about the troubles we have faced and we have learned how to give those to you to deal with. We have learned that every lesson was designed with our righteousness and purity in mind. We have learned that everything you do and speak is because you love me so much that you sent your very son to die on Earth so that I might be able to have a relationship with you and so that I can go to heaven and be with you forever. Lord, be with me as I walk these lessons out according to your will. Be my strength when I am weak. Be my living water when I am thirsty. Continue to show me that I am truly Your Beloved Child and put people in my life to support these truths. In Jesus' mighty name. Amen.

Galatians 6:9: "Let us not become weary in doing good, for at a proper time we will reap a harvest if we do not give up."

Romans 8:25: "But if we hope for what we do not have, we wait for it patiently."

1 Corinthians 15:58: " Therefore, my beloved brothers, be steadfast, immovable, always abounding in the work of the Lord, knowing that in the Lord your labor is not in vain."

1 John 3:2: "Beloved, we are God's children now and what we will be has not yet appeared, but we know that when He appears we shall be like Him because we shall see Him as He is."

www.ingramcontent.com/pod-product-compliance
Lightning Source LLC
Chambersburg PA
CBHW071513120626
46550CB00006B/2207